C.I.H. Ness

The Oriental or Arabian Art of Charming Horses and Breaking Colts

Containing full instructions for raising, training, riding, driving, stabling, feeding, and doctoring horses

C.I.H. Ness

The Oriental or Arabian Art of Charming Horses and Breaking Colts
Containing full instructions for raising, training, riding, driving, stabling, feeding, and doctoring horses

ISBN/EAN: 9783744793223

Printed in Europe, USA, Canada, Australia, Japan

Cover: Foto ©ninafisch / pixelio.de

More available books at **www.hansebooks.com**

THE ORIENTAL OR ARABIAN ART

OF

CHARMING HORSES

AND

BREAKING COLTS.

CONTAINING

FULL INSTRUCTIONS FOR RAISING, TRAINING, RIDING,
DRIVING, STABLING, FEEDING, AND
DOCTORING HORSES.

By C. I. H. NESS, M.D.,
VETERINARIAN AND TRAINER.

CINCINNATI, OHIO:
PUBLISHED BY THE AUTHOR.
1861.

INTRODUCTORY REMARKS.

The Horse is the most noble and the most useful of the domestic animals. It is only in a few localities, and under a few circumstances, that any other beast of burden can compare with him for usefulness; while for gracefulness and speed of motion, and for beauty and symmetry of form, the ox, the camel, the ass, the mule, the elephant, are all completely and forever eclipsed.

I need offer no other apology, then, for presenting to the public this little volume—the result of over twenty years' experience in the raising, breaking, training and educating of this *animal*. Also, some ten years' experience in medicine and surgery on this *noble* animal.

Let none say I have misled them by my title. I shall give you all there is of the Oriental or Arabian art of charming horses. If what *they* call magic is only the practice of scientific principles, that is no fault of mine. It is the fault or the blindness of the Orientals themselves, in attributing to magic, or supernatural agency, that which can be, and is performed by natural means; and it is our fault if we believe such antiquated superstitions.

Nor is it any deception to designate the method of training vicious horses and colts, as set forth in this pamphlet, by the term *charming*, (or power of mind.) Charming may be practiced by natural, as well as supernatural means; and there is no doubt but the Arabians and other Orientalists did all their charming on precisely the principle herein set forth, though they pretended it was done by supernatural means, and though they might have been innocent in the belief that their success in taming the wild and vicious horse committed to their charge depended on the particular terms of jargon which they whispered in his ear.

Nor do I practice any unwarrantable deception when I promise to teach you the Oriental or Arabian art of taming wild and vicious horses. I will not only do this, but I will rob it of its antiquated mysticisms, absurdities, and difficulties.

I will show you what has heretofore been considered difficult and complicated, can be explained on natural principles, and is easy to the comprehension and practice of every owner of a horse.

The truth is, that *noble* animal (the HORSE) has been misunderstood and much abused. By many he has not been treated as an animal, but rather as a stick of timber, which could be hewn with an ax, or molded by the chisel into any desirable shape; or as a block of marble, tumbled along through the streets to the workshop of the artist, to be by him hammered, chiseled, cut, and carved into an equestrian statue.

If we succeed in establishing the claims of the horse to an animal nature, and show how he may be most successfully subdued and rendered useful to man, we shall claim, whether we receive it or not, more credit than the charmers of the Orient received, who shrouded the science in a vail of mystery, while they left the astonished beholders of their performances untaught and unenlightened in the *modus operandi* of their pretended divinations.

THE AUTHOR.

PART I.

THE ORIENTAL ART THE TRUE PHILOSOPHY.

We have often read of the wonderful power which the Arabs and other Orientals have over the horse; of their taking them wild from the native forests, and, by supernatural, or magic influence, training them not only to the common purposes of usefulness, but teaching them the greatest possible variety of feats, tricks, and wonderful performances; of their whispering to the horse, as if he possessed the spirit of some departed worthy, and they were in confidence consulting and communicating with him. We have read, too, of the "Black Art," and the astounding miracles said to be performed by its means. We have seen persons, even in this enlightened age, who profess to believe in it; nay, more, we once met a livery-stable loafer who undertook to palm himself off on us as a thorough practitioner of this art, (?) and offered his services, at a round price, in the business of charming, conquering and subduing the wildest and most ungovernable horses that might be brought to him for that purpose. Those who will believe such wild and superstitious notions, need themselves to be tamed and instructed into the first principles of modern science, and they deserve no pity if they are occasionally most essentially humbugged.

But that the Arabians, and many Europeans and Americans, have been wonderfully successful in breaking colts, taming vicious and ungovernable horses, and teaching them a great variety of tricks and performances, is an undisputed truth; and that the manner of doing this is well worthy of being called an art, is equally true.

Who that has witnessed the astonishing performances of this noble animal in the circus, but has, at times, almost attributed it to the possession of the human intellect; and all will admit that the instinct and tractability of the horse are of the highest order of the brute creation. Yet such power over the horse—and we had almost said any horse, but there is as much difference in horses as in men—can be possessed by any one who will practice a few plain and simple rules.

What, then, is the Arabian or Black Art of charming horses? We think it may be summed up in a few words, *kindness, patience, and perseverance.* The Arabian has all these, and, in addition, what too many in this country of luxury and extravagance do not have—an abundance of time. The Arabian, and those who have pretended to practice the Black Art, are in the habit of spending much time in the company of the horse. They ride, brush, curry, caress, fondle, talk, whistle, and sing to the horse, and, what too many are never known to do, love this noble animal. By these various and continued means, they obtain a wonderful power over any one of the race that may be placed under their charge. It matters but little to the horse whether his master whistles Yankee Doodle, or the tune the old cow died on, as long as he appears pleasant. Yet we think, in speaking to a horse, we should speak plain and distinct; also, with a gesture, that he may understand what we want, if not what we say, not forgetting our mind influences his; although I believe the horse understands many words spoken to or about him, quite as readily as a small child.

We assert, then, and without fear of contradiction, that the whole secret of training horses, whether practiced by Arabians, Gipsies, Black Art performers, livery-stable loungers, or the worthy and honorable horseman, lies in perseverance, kind and patient instruction, not forgetting the power that man has over the brute creation. *Use, but not abuse it.* We will try to throw more light on this subject as we progress with our little work.

How to make a Horse Pace.

Take some lead balls, weighing from two to three ounces, with a hole through each; string enough on a cord to go round the fetlock. Tie a string around the right fore-foot and the left hind-foot; ride him slow; when he becomes used to this, change them, putting them on the opposite feet. *Patience and perseverance will move mountains.*

How to cure a Horse from interfering.

Pare the inside of the hoof the lowest, and make the inside of the shoe the heaviest; if this does not cure him, I do not know of anything that will, as I have tried many others in vain.

How to Shoe Horses.

A saddle horse should be shod with a smooth, spring heel shoe; a buggy horse with heel corks, while the coach horse should have toe corks as well as heels on his hind feet; heels with no toe corks on the forward feet. In shoeing your dray, cart, or wagon horse, do not forget to have low but heavy corks all round, toes and heels. Blacksmiths generally make their nails too large; do not pare the heels much, as it will tend to strain the heel cords; make the shoe to fit the foot, not pare the foot to fit the shoe; let the rim of the hoof rest on the shoe; do not cut the front of the hoof so as to make the foot stump-toed; let the hoof be as flat as possible; if the shoe rests on the pith, it will cause corns; if there are any corns, cut them out, and dress with spirits turpentine; fill the cavity with tar or resin, melt in with a hot iron; be careful not to point your nail in; and, as you may lame the horse, be careful your nails do not break, and the stub turn in while the point may come out; if this should occur, it would be very painful to the horse.

Early Training.

As horses are mainly valuable for their utility to man, it is apparent that the full development of the physical system of the animal is not all that needs to be secured, though that is necessarily the primary department, upon which all else is to be based. The best-developed animal might be so vicious as to be entirely valueless; though it is a rule, that development of form and of disposition correspond to each other.

Yet the horse being one of the most intelligent of the animal creation, and easily trained into objectionable as well as desirable habits, it behooves every one having the care of young horses and colts, to guard carefully the influences brought to bear upon their disposition. The usual custom throughout the West has been to let them run wild almost, until three or four years old, and then put them through—not a regular system of "breaking,"—but such exercises as the disposition of the master might dictate at the moment, and which often exhibited far more of the spleen and irritability, impatience and violence of temper of the man, than of care for the horse. Almost the first experience of life the colt gets, after he has learned the use of his legs, is a pelting with small stones, clods, sticks, or switches, from mischievous boys, who delight in his infantile antics to avoid his persecutors; and thus, from the first, he learns to look upon man as an enemy to be dreaded and avoided, while evil disposings to kick, strike, etc., and ill-nature generally, are forced upon him. Age and strength accumulate, and with them ill-treatment, (for the amusement of its masters it may be, or by virtue of their thoughtless disregard of causes and effects,) until, when large and old enough to become serviceable, the difficult and dangerous process of "breaking" becomes necessary. And it too often happens, that when this is well done, as all admit it should be, the horse is really broken, and has lost all that spirit and nobleness so much admired in this truly noble animal. The whole idea of "breaking" implies, in fact, a necessary evil, is part of the same philosophy which once made our school-houses depositories of birch, and theaters of tragic cruelty; a philosophy which, thanks to enlightened progress, is rapidly passing away.

The colt should be accustomed to kindness, and gentle, yet firm handling, from the first, and in this manner learn perfect obedience to his master's will. The halter may, indeed should be, placed upon him when quite young, and he should learn to be guided by it in any direction, and with ease; and as he grows up, one lesson after another may be added, as the owner's wishes or fancy may dictate, until, when the time comes that his services are demanded, he is ready trained for the service, educated in the way he should go, and will walk therein. The whole process should be one of careful avoidance of influences tending to create bad habits, teaching the animal what it will be required to know, before that requisition comes, and by education supersede the necessity for the unphilosophical and often brutal "breaking."

The advantages of careful training during growth are many and important. It affords the best possible means of developing the animal in every respect; keeps him under the constant care of the owner, and induces him to think and reason upon what he does; creates a sympathy, so to term it, between them, which elevates the character of both. It prevents the vicious habits usually engendered from carelessness of the owner, and which cannot always be eradicated, and avoids the cruelty and abuse of "breaking." The horse may be made tractable, reliable, and safe, without having his energy and spirit crushed out of him; and he may be noble, active, and proud in his movements, without being restive, irritable, and treacherous, and, as a consequence, will be more easily kept in fine condition and good health. It is only a continuation of the principles of breeding, extended to the full development of the animal, here advocated; and, while all cannot be equally successful in this, as in any other of the pursuits of life, all will be more successful, and richly rewarded for their efforts to attain it. The principal reasons for the general untrained character of horses, seems to be the lack of any systematic effort at training, and the uncontrolled passions of those who have the handling and care of horses. It is no uncommon thing to see angry bipeds venting their passion upon unoffending animals, as the most convenient recipient of their ire. And such scenes are not confined to the street, the highway, or the farm; but are found in all. The effects are mischievous, and ruinous to the best interests of the owner, because injuring and depreciating in value his property in the market. Horse education, really, is a marketable commodity, and may be, indeed always is, estimated in dollars and cents.

Taming a vicious Horse.

In nine cases out of ten, those who undertake to tame a vicious horse do the very things they ought not to do, while the things they ought to do they do not.

While in the city of Boston, in the year 1848, I was, in company with several others, shown a beautiful spotted horse, about eight years old, and well worth, if faultless, one hundred and fifty dollars, which it was said by the honest salesman no man could ride, or drive in a chaise, (a two-wheel vehicle much used formerly at the east.) Mr. A—— said he would try him, and gave sixty dollars for the noble animal, which could not have been purchased for twice that sum, had he borne a reputation for good behavior.

He led the horse home, about eight miles from the city, by the side of another, put him in the stable, fed him, and retired for the night. The next morning he went to the stable "to break the d——d horse, or his own neck," to use his own expression. As he approached the horse, he remarked, in a somewhat triumphant and defiant tone: "So, ho! you are the fellow that allows no one to straddle your back, are you? We'll see whether you can shake me off as easy as you have some others; if you do, you will be the first horse that ever shook me from his back."

It really seemed as if the horse knew the substance of the remarks made in his hearing, by the motion of his head, the manner in which he stepped from one side of the stall to the other, and various other indications of uneasiness and suspicion. At any rate, whether he comprehended the language of his new master or not, he evidently did not like the *tone* of his voice, nor the *swaggering* of his person. A horse learns the different inflections of the human voice sooner than many a school-boy.

Our hero now led the horse from the stable, put a saddle upon his back, buckled it with uncommon tightness, and after trying the stirrups to see that all was sound and right, with a single bound was in the saddle.

Now commenced a scene of rearing, and springing, and pitching unlike anything I ever before witnessed. In retaliation, the rider commenced using the cowhide freely over the rump, about the sides and legs of the animal, and, at length, over his head, eyes, ears, and mouth. It was evidently a battle between two equally determined, but unequally powerful opponents—a trial of animal strength—an exhibition of dexterity on the part of the animal, to throw off the disagreeable load; on the part of the disagreeable load—the man—to conquer, to subdue, to maintain his position. But the horse, being the stouter of the two, was the victor, and would have thrown his load a rod at least from his back, but for the rider's foot having caught in the stirrup; and in the plight, the horse would soon have kicked his brains out, if he had any, but for the interference and assistance of the bystanders, who soon liberated the prisoner from his critical situation.

But was this horse broken? No. But the owner was, from any future attempts to ride a vicious horse.

One of the spectators of this scene asked the owner of the animal what he would take for him. Being taken in just the mood for selling cheap, he replied: "Anything you please." A bargain was soon struck up, and the horse changed hands for fifty dollars. The crowd was making tracks to follow the horse to the stable of the new owner, but the latter observed that he should make no attempt to ride him at present, and when he did, he should by no means allow any one to be present on the occasion.

Three weeks after this, I, with many others in the village which was now the new home of this "vicious horse," had the pleasure of seeing this gentleman (for though he was what is termed a horse-jockey, he was a *gentle*-man in his treatment of horses) pass through the place gracefully riding the back of this noble, but heretofore proscribed animal, with apparently as much pleasure to the horse as to the rider. There was no springing, rearing, or whipping; but the horse and the rider moved up and down the main thoroughfare of the village, in the presence of hundreds of excited spectators, as if they were a part of each other.

How was this miraculous change brought about? I will give you the horse tamer's own account of the matter, as nearly as my memory will serve at this distant period of time; which, however, is uncommonly distinct, for the circumstance made an indelible impression on my mind, as it constituted my first valuable lesson in the "Oriental Art of Charming Horses."

"I took my horse home," said he, "and spent several days in forming an acquaintance with him. I might have succeeded in riding him sooner, but then, I am very formal about such matters—I want to be regularly introduced to a horse—a coquettish, shy, non-committal, bashful, nervous, excitable, egotistical, joking, frolicksome, quick-tempered, vicious, or lazy horse, (for horses have as great a variety of characteristics as men, or women either,) as regularly introduced as to one whom I might choose for a partner in business, or a partner at the altar. I want then to become intimately acquainted—go through a regular courtship—that we may love each other; for I will never own a horse that I can not love.

"But, as I was saying, I took my horse home, put him in a clean, nice stable, fed him with the best I had, brushed him, combed him, conversed with him, caressed him myself—I never have a *servant* to do my courting for me. We soon became the best of friends. I can always tell when I am getting the right side of a horse. At first he was shy—treated me with coolness—then became too familiar by half. I put on my best countenance, and talked to him in my most wooing tones; I succeeded in making him know me, love me, and fear me. I say fear me, for I whipped him—I whip horses as I do children—never in anger, always from a sense of duty; and I take immediate steps to let the animal know why I whip him, and how painful it is for me to do so.

"At length I led him into the center of the stable, placed a saddle gently across his back, and then went to his head and caressed him. I was a long time adjusting the saddle to suit me, for my time was principally occupied in winning the affection of the horse. At length, all things ready, I crawled shyly upon his back, setting down so easily that he could scarcely distinguish the time when I was fairly fixed; my head mean time, and for some time afterward, close to his. I made no motion for him to go, but slipped off, and went for a pair of mittens, though it was July; put on the mittens and again mounted his back cautiously—no, not cautiously, for it will never do to be *cautious*, but in a friendly, familiar manner, as much as to say, I have a right to a place on your back, but, then, it is with your leave, sir. After turning him around once by the bridle, I was again off to get my hat, then my whip, etc., and finally took off his saddle and put him back into his stall. This I did several times, perhaps more times than was necessary, but I was in no hurry.

"I next took him into the yard, and jumping upon another horse, rode several times around him, then left that and mounted him, and rode several times around the first horse. This was a great feat—it was 'glory enough for one day;' I therefore put the horse up and left him for a day.

"The next day I tried both horses again, but rode a longer time than the first day. Again, I ventured still further, riding around my house, then down the road to the brook and back, until, finally, I can take a journey on the best saddle horse I ever owned, which cost me but *fifty dollars.*"

Now who will say that horses have not sense? Who will say that they must not be treated, at least as we would treat a dog, or a cat, or a bird, that we would wish to tame and instruct?

Teaching a Horse various Tricks.

Almost any horse can be taught to perform tricks, but some horses are more tractable than others. You must select a good shaped, bright-eyed, nimble, playful horse, not too large, nor too stoutly built. Some horses are made only to work, and others only to be lazy. Neither of these should be selected as a trick horse. If you are any judge of horses, your own judgment, better than a page of directions, will enable you to pick out your horse. He should also be healthy; it is waste time to teach a cripple that which he can not perform well, if at all.

Now, presuming you have the right kind of a horse, observe strictly the following rules all through:

1st. Never treat your horse with anything but kindness. You may have a whip, and crack and snap it; occasionally use it to good purpose around your horses' legs. He will soon learn whether you do it because you are his master, have a right to use it, and do not use it with cruelty, or whether you are unreasonable, bad tempered, and impatient.

2d. Never allow any one to feed, curry, or take any other care of your horse; or, if you must occasionally commit him to other hands, they should be charged not to notice him, or play with him, but be as indifferent as possible in their treatment of him. Your horse should learn that no one loves him or cares for him but yourself. You should endeavor, by every possible method, to impress him with the idea that he is *your* horse, *your* pet, *your* friend, and must do all these things which you are teaching him just for *your* gratification alone.

3d. Never allow any other horse, animal, child, or man to be present while you are giving instruction. After he has become familiar with his lessons and performs them well; after you are satisfied and *he* is satisfied, that the thing is well done, then you may venture to introduce one spectator, then two, a dozen, or a thousand. But undertake no *new* trick in presence of spectators.

4th. Never undertake more than one thing at a time. However simple that thing may be, let your horse become familiar and dexterous in that before confusing him with anything else.

5th. When your horse has performed well, always caress, fondle, and feed him. Put your head up to his, and your arm around his neck, and tell him he is a fine boy, and shall have the best oats that can be had in market. He may not know the meaning of your words, but you can not say all this to a horse, without doing it in just the manner which indicates to him your affections, interest, and approval. This is just the very thing wanted. This is precisely the Oriental art of charming horses. It is to win his favor, excite his pride and ambition, enlist his affections. A horse, and, indeed, for that matter, nearly all animals, have all the affections and instincts of man, and they only want to be appealed to, and enlisted in your behalf, when they will be ten times more obedient to your wishes, and subservient to your demands, than the most abject office-seeker is to the President, the Governor, or the "Dear People."

Now, if you have picked out your horse, and will observe the above rules, you may begin by taking a handkerchief, and placing it in a certain part of the stable; then, pointing to the handkerchief, say, "Bring me that handkerchief, sir," leading the horse to it, (first presuming, however, that he has seen and smelled of it twenty times before,) bearing his head toward it, and, at the same time, lifting it up to his mouth. Put it into his mouth; if he is disposed to drop it, hold it to his mouth, and lead him to the other side of the stable and put it down. Now take the handkerchief and carry it back to where you put it first, then come back to the horse and say as before, (in fact, *always* use the same expression and in the same tone of voice,) "Bring me that handkerchief, sir;" if he does not start for it, lead him as before, and pass through the whole ceremony precisely as the first time. The third or fourth time, you can venture to snap your whip and manifest some signs of displeasure, but finish with a friendly gesture and word, and again lead him to the object, and go through the whole round of ceremony. He will, at length, go so far as to go and take the handkerchief in his mouth, and then, from pure mischief, perhaps, shake it about, or carry it anywhere else but where you want him to. Then snap your whip, and again make him carry it to the place where you were standing or sitting. Follow this up and you will soon learn your horse to bring your handkerchief to you without your moving from your position; then your hat, gloves, or any other object.

If it is a pail, and he takes hold of it by its side instead of the handle, go to him, take it from his mouth, and put the handle in his mouth, saying, "That is not right, sir; this is the way!" Some such expression as this should be always used, and always in precisely the same way, when he does not perform correctly, and he will soon learn what is meant by it, if applied to any other transaction improperly performed.

You can now go on and teach your horse anything you please. You can teach him to go and bring your cows or sheep for you; and though he will not learn it as readily, nor be as serviceable for that purpose as a well-trained dog, yet the novelty of the transaction well repays for the extra trouble that is taken.

It is by such means that a circus horse is taught to lie down or sit up; hold up one foot or the other at command; shake his head, as if to say No, and nod his head as if to say Yes, to any question; to turn half way or all the way around, and remain in that position until he hears a certain word. To pick out the letters of the alphabet, and spell, not any word, but such words as he has been taught to spell. There is, in fact nothing which you may not teach a horse to do, if you will. But you must observe strictly the above rules. Any one else tampering with your horse, and directing him in a little different way, causes him to mistake, and he is as sensitive of the mistake as a man would be, and will not like to try it again.

How to make a Horse lie down.

Everything that we want to teach the horse must be commenced in some way to give him an idea of what you want him to do, and then be repeated till he learns it perfectly. To make a horse lie down, bend his left fore leg, and slip a loop over it, so that he cannot get it down. Then put a circingle around his body, and fasten one end of a long strap around the other fore leg, just above the hoof. Place the other end under the circingle, so as to keep the strap in the right hand; stand on the left side of the horse, grasp the bit in your left hand, pull steadily on the strap with your right; bear against his shoulder till you cause him to move. As soon as he lifts his weight, your pulling will raise the other foot, and he will have to come on his knees. Keep the strap tight in your hand, so that he cannot straighten his leg if he raises up. Hold him in his position, and turn his head toward you; bear against his side with your shoulder, not hard, but with a steady, equal pressure, and in about ten minutes he will lie down. As soon as he lies down he will be completely conquered, and you can handle him as you please. Take off the straps, and straighten out his legs; rub him lightly about the face and neck with your hand the way the hair lays; handle all his legs, and after he has lain ten or twenty minutes, let him get up again. After resting him a short time, make him lie down as before. Repeat the operation three or four times, which will be sufficient for one lesson. Give him two lessons a day, and when you have given him four lessons, he will lie down by taking hold of one foot. As soon as he is well broken to lie down in this way, tap him on the opposite leg with a stick when you take hold of his foot, and in a few days he will lie down from the mere motion of the stick.

How to make a Horse follow you.

Turn him into a large stable or shed, where there is no chance to get out, with a halter or bridle on. Go to him and gentle him a little, take hold of his halter and turn him toward you, at the same time touching him lightly over the hips with a long whip. Lead him the length of the stable, rubbing him on the neck, saying, in a steady tone of voice, as you lead him, COME ALONG, BOY! or use his name instead of boy, if you choose. Every time you turn, touch him slightly with the whip, to make him step up close to you, and then caress him with your hand. He will soon learn to hurry up to escape the whip and be caressed, and you can make him follow you around without taking hold of the halter. If he should stop and turn from you, give him a few cuts about the hind legs, and he will soon turn his head toward you, when you must always caress him. A few lessons of this kind will make him run after you, when he sees the motion of the whip—in twenty or thirty minutes he will follow you about the stable. After you have given him two or three lessons in the stable, take him out into a small lot and train him; and from thence you can take him into the road and make him follow you anywhere, and run after you.

Breaking Colts.

There is a great difference in colts, and consequently some will, of necessity, be harder to break than others.

But the methods are the same in *nature* with all colts. Some will require much more time and patience than others; but whatever the amount of time, it is of no use for you to fret, worry, swear, and rave at them. For every minute spent in raving at them, you will have to spend ten in gentleness, kindness, and patience afterward. It is seldom that a colt *must* be tamed on the very day you at first select, and when you or they are likely to get out of patience, it is better to postpone operations till another time.

The first thing is to approach him, in the stable, or a small inclosure, in a familiar, friendly manner, with nothing in your hand, and no person or animal in sight. As you approach, extend one hand toward him and commence talking to him in a low tone of voice. Speak plain and pleasant, keep talking; a horse loves a person that has much to say, if he is good-natured; call him by some endearing name, as you can not do this without showing your friendship for him.

As you draw near the horse or colt, if he turns from you, stop until he stops and has taken another look at you. He will then allow you to approach still nearer. If he again starts, stop yourself again. It is of no use to follow him while he is in motion. He can move faster than you can, and will only widen the distance between you. When he finds you have not hurt him by being within two rods of him, he may let you come within a rod and a half. If you can not get up to his head and take hold of it within fifteen or twenty minutes, better postpone the attempt for an hour or two, or longer, at convenience.

When you have succeeded in reaching his head, pat him on the neck, put your head close to his, and talk to him, and he will soon be pleased with the familiarity. If you are not in too great haste, it is better to do this with him frequently, before approaching him with anything in your hand.

So much being accomplished, you can now approach him with a halter, whip, or anything else; but if he turns from you, do not follow him up. Leave him and again go with nothing in your hand. Be exceedingly careful you do not lose favor with him; if you do, you must begin all over again. Once his friend, never let him suppose you are or can be his enemy.

After you have fondled with him several times with a whip, halter, harness, or anything else you please, take a leather halter (in no case use a rope halter) and put it to his nose, then rub it on his neck, around his head, mouth, and nose, being careful always not to approach too near his eyes. Do this frequently before putting it over his head. When you get ready, put it over his head so easily and with so much unconcern, that he will not know you have any designs in doing it. Do not attempt *now* to fasten it, unless he is very tame and submissive. Take another opportunity.

After your colt has become used to the feeling of the halter, you can then lead him about; but if he falls back, go up to him and pat him on the neck. Don't let him have a chance to try his strength; if you do, he will find out that he is stronger than you are. This neither a colt nor a horse ever ought to know. When you have succeeded thus far with him, and you and he have had no "falling out," you can go on step by step, making him familiar, by degrees, with every kind of service to which he is liable to be called.

Every colt should be made familiar with drums, fifes,

horns, railroad cars; and with various colors and objects. But never approach them or look at them while making any uncommon noise for the purpose of breaking them. Whatever you do in this line, should be done, at first, at a distance, until the colt cares nothing about it; then approach a step nearer. Avoid all *sudden* frights. I once knew a young horse to be so badly frightened at the noise and sudden motion of a company of children coming out of a school-room, that he would shy off the track for months if two or three children passed him on the road. I have known horses to be equally frightened at a rail car. It is better to pasture them, if possible, near, but not too near, a railroad track, and then in a lot adjoining a track. If you can not do this, the first opportunity you can have, take them near, but again, not too near, a railroad track. Next time a little nearer, always letting them *see* the cars as they pass. Colts that are properly trained to familiarity with all such things as they are likely to see and hear, will never afterward be frightened while in the harness. Of course most of the above applies only to colts that are very skittish.

Kicking.

This is generally brought on by boys tampering with the legs of the horse, or by poultry running around his legs and annoying him, or by the reins, etc., getting under his tail or around his legs while on the road. Prevention here, as in all other bad habits, is worth more than cure. It is a very difficult matter to break a horse of the habit of kicking at every little annoyance, when once the habit is confirmed.

Kicking against the sides of the stall can generally be prevented by attaching thorns to the sides of the stall, or anything that will prickle without injuring the feet. Kicking in the harness is best conquered by stout straps, so adjusted as to prevent his raising his hind feet. The strap must be very strong and a little springy, and then, it must be resorted to more for the purpose of preventing the horse from breaking the carriage, than with any expectation of reforming him.

The best plan is to begin early with your colt; or, if your colt is already a horse, then begin at once a thorough system of training, to get him used to various annoyances by degrees, and with kind treatment, as in the manner herein recommended for putting on the bridle. Any horse can be taught to disregard the reins getting under his tail, or the foot-board coming up against him, just as easily as he can be reconciled to the saddle or the bits. All such things are an annoyance to the horse or colt, when first submitted to. The drum and fife, and other musical instruments are an annoyance; so also the railroad car and the steam whistle. We *train* our horses to such things—then why not train them to everything with which they are likely to be annoyed. Any man who does not love a horse well enough, or who does not take enough pride in him to guard him in the first four years of his life against the dangers of the future, should never own a horse. He should at once adopt some branch of business that will enable him to get along without a horse, and forever afterward resort to the railroad car and the steamboat.

How to catch Colts in the Pastures or Prairies.

If they are very wild or shy, two or even three should be employed to go on all sides and gradually approach them. Do not look directly at them, nor approach in a direct line, nor raise the hands as if to head them off. You must not let them mistrust that you want to catch them. Let one who is on a horse approach slowly, and if your horse will nibble the grass, let him do so a minute, and then take a step nearer; by such means you can soon go in among them, and after your horse has smelled of them and they of him, then turn toward your home, and in most cases they will follow into the barn yard. If they will not do it at first, perseverance will always succeed. It is sometimes well, but not always necessary, to feed them.

Avoid all haste, noise, flurry, and excitement. If you get out of patience, do not let your colts know it; if you do, you will have lost all your labor thus far. If you can not control yourself in this matter, it is doubtful whether you can control the colts after you catch them. I firmly believe that the wildest prairie colt may be caught without the lasso or the trap, if one has sufficient patience, and exercises a little dexterity and prudence.

Slipping the Halter.

Some horses are very dexterous at this, and almost always succeed in getting loose in the stable, keeping other horses awake, and endangering their own limbs to the kicks of others, besides other evils.

The web of the halter should be made so as to slip only one way; or a strap may be buckled around the neck, and attached to the halter just tight enough not to injure or annoy him, but to prevent his slipping it off.

Restlessness while being shod.

If a young horse is unwilling to be shod, he should be allowed to see several others go through the operation before taking his turn. This, with other means of gentleness, will generally succeed. But if not, then it will be necessary to put your horse through a regular course of training—to do, in fact, what should have been done before he was ever sent to be shod at all.

Take his foot up frequently and hold it as the smith does, until he cares nothing about it, then hammer it, and do whatever else will be an imitation of the process of shoeing. By such means your horse will be prepared for an operation which would otherwise be strange to him. A horse does not refuse to be shod from mere bad temper; it is because he does not know what you want to do with his foot, or he has been roughly handled, badly trained, or previously maimed by some careless smith.

To prevent rolling in the Stall.

This is a very dangerous habit, and can be prevented only by tying the horse so that he can lie down, but not touch his head to the floor. This is very tiresome to the horse, and hence, if you care enough for his comfort and health, build a narrow platform, eighteen to twenty-four inches in width, slanting at an angle of thirty to forty degrees, so that it will form a pillow for his head and neck; then adjust a rope so that as he lies down, his head will naturally rest on the platform or pillow. He will not roll, unless he can get his head as low as the floor of the stable.

How to break Horses from balking.

In the first place never teach your horse to balk, by giving him a greater load than he can carry, or requiring him to go up too steep a hill without permitting him to stop. If you tell him to stop, in going up a steep hill, it is better than to allow him to do it of his own accord. If he finds he can stop of his own will, and start when he pleases, he will soon learn to do it when he ought not to. If at any time he stops without your stopping him, give him a sharp cut, and make him go on, even if you think he ought to stop at that very place; but soon yourself give him an opportunity to stop. This will teach him that he is to stop only at your will, and that you are not unreasonable in your demands. I believe that all balky horses are in the first instance taught to balk by their careless and inconsiderate owners, who overload them, and allow them to stop or go according to their own will. Once a horse finds he can stop at will without reproof, he will stop, perhaps on a smooth road, or in the middle of a village, or on the street of a city, where you will be mortified as well as discommoded.

But what shall we do with a horse who has thoroughly learned to balk, and whom whipping only hardens? Desperate remedies should sometimes be used for desperate cases, and you may in such cases either kill your horse as not being worthy the oats you give him, or you may fasten him to a strong carriage, put on a strong harness and reins, and seating yourself firmly in the vehicle, drive on; if he balks, set fire to a bunch of shavings or a newspaper at his heels, or a bunch of fire-crackers; he is bound to go in such case—perhaps too fast for you—but of this you must run your risk. It is a desperate remedy, but when kindness and good treatment do not succeed, such a remedy will succeed better, and is more humane than beating, unmerciful whipping, etc., which seldom succeed at all.

Crib Biting.

This is a bad habit, and very annoying to the owner of a horse. Various remedies have been tried, such as ironing the manger, partitions, etc. I know of no certain cure but an iron muzzle, with bars just wide enough apart to allow the horse to pick up his grain and draw out his hay with his tongue, but not to get hold of anything with his teeth. If this habit is not broken it will soon be imitated by every horse in the stable.

To make a Horse lie down at Night.

Horses that never lie down when they sleep will not do as well as those who are in the habit of it. They perhaps are afraid of being caught by the halter, or they have already been cast in the night, and do not like to try it again. Such horses should be let loose in a stable at night, or in a large stall, without being tied, and furnished with a tempting bed, until the habit of lying down is acquired, and the fear of it removed.

Unwillingness to be mounted.

In some this is mere playfulness, while in others it is a decided unwillingness to be driven. Give such horses as the former more hay and less oats, and never let them start immediately on your mounting them or getting into the carriage. A systematic and persevering course of such treatment will, in the end, usually teach the horse that you are not ready for him to go the instant you touch your foot to the stirrup, but you have gloves or mittens to put on, or your reins to adjust, and it is useless for him to be in a hurry.

But if it is because he does *not* want to go, then it may be he wants more oats and less hay; or he has been perhaps badly used when out on former occasions. In either case, however, whipping does no good; indeed I am satisfied that for all viciousness in horses, whipping does no good, but only aggravates the evil. An occasional sharp crack with the whip, followed by tones of friendship familiar to the horse, will generally do good; but if your horse has never heard you use such tones, then you had better sell him at once, and get a horse without bad habits—some drone which has not life enough in him to be restless, and not strength enough to kick.

Running away.

The best way to cure this, if it is a settled habit, is to get your horse on a good road, and if he starts, let him go, and the moment he slacks give him a sharp cut with the whip, until he has had as much running as he wants.

Restiveness.

This is one of the worst manifestations in the horse. It is the result of bad management in the early training of the horse, and when once a settled habit, it becomes dangerous to any but the best rider or driver to attempt his management. Whipping, hallooing, jerking and yanking with the bridle only make the matter worse. If you can not soothe such a horse by kind treatment, you had better give him up as a hopeless case.

Biting.

This is generally the result of allowing boys to "fool" with a horse, by pointing sticks at him; though sometimes the cause is in the natural disposition of the horse. Here again, whipping is of no use. Stewart says, he has seen horses whipped till nearly dead, but to no effect. If you can obtain something exceedingly disagreeable to the taste of a horse, as some very bitter herb, saturate a piece of cloth and wind it around a stick for him to bite at; it will often, in connection with kind treatment, have a tendency to break him. A single sharp cut of the whip across the mouth on the instant, will sometimes do good; but unmerciful whipping, raving, swearing—never.

The Author's fancy for a Trick Horse.

Color is quite immaterial, otherwise than to please the eye; a thorough-bred is best—a half-blood will do—about fifteen or sixteen hands high. Be sure he or she is sound in body, limbs, and wind; head, neck, and withers high; wide between the eyes; large and red nostrils; top of the neck small; ears small and well set forward; active; eyes large and full; countenance bright and intelligent; mane and foretop good length; tail medium and natural length, carried up well when he or she moves; medium-sized and sound dark hoofs;

fetlock joints springy; proud and bold in look and movement; clean taper limbs, with good muscle; a mare or stallion would be preferable; the less he or she has been handled the better; age, two or three years.

[I have spoken on this subject before, but owing to a request of some of my friends, I have here given a more perfect description, so one not being a judge of horses can select a trick horse.—THE AUTHOR.]

A FEW REMARKS ON THE COLT,

TAKEN FROM OTHER AUTHORS.

How to Succeed in Getting the Colt from Pasture.

Go to the pasture and walk around the whole herd quietly, and at such a distance as not to cause them to scare and run. Then approach them very slowly, and if they stick up their heads and seem to be frightened, hold on until they become quiet, so as not to make them run before you are close enough to drive them in the direction you want to go. And when you begin to drive, do not flourish your arms or halloo, but gently follow them off, leaving the direction free for them that you wish them to take. Thus taking advantage of their ignorance, you will be able to get them in the pound as easily as the hunter drives the quails into his net. For, if they have always run into the pasture uncared for, (as many horses do in prairie countries and on large plantations,) there is no reason why they should not be as wild as the sportsman's birds, and require the same gentle treatment, if you want to get them without trouble; for the horse, in his natural state, is as wild as any of the undomesticated animals, though more easily tamed than most of them.

How to stable a Colt without Trouble.

The next step will be, to get the horse into a stable or shed. This should be done as quietly as possible, so as not to excite any suspicion in the horse of any danger befalling him. The best way to do this, is to lead a gentle horse into the stable first and hitch him, then quietly walk around the colt and let him go in of his own accord. It is almost impossible to get men who have never practiced on this principle, to go slow and considerate about it. They do not know that in handling a wild horse, above all other things, is that good old adage true, that "haste makes waste;" that is, waste of time, for the gain of trouble and perplexity.

One wrong move may frighten your horse, and make him think it is necessary to escape at all hazards for the safety of his life, and thus make two hours' work of a ten minutes' job; and this would be all your own fault, and entirely unnecessary, for he will not run unless you run after him, and that would not be good policy, unless you knew that you could outrun him; or you will have to let him stop of his own accord after all. But he will not try to break away, unless you attempt to force him into measures. If he does not see the way at once, and is a little fretful about going in, do not undertake to drive him, but give him a little less room outside, by gently closing in around him. Do not raise your arms, but let them hang at your side, for you might as well raise a club. The horse has never studied anatomy, and does not know but they will unhinge themselves and fly at him. If he attempts to turn back, walk before him, but do not run; and if he gets past you, encircle him again in the same quiet manner, and he will soon find that you are not going to hurt him; and you can soon walk so close around him that he will go into the stable for more room, and to get further from you. As soon as he is in, remove the quiet horse and shut the door. This will be his first notion of confinement, not knowing how to get in such a place, nor how to get out of it. That he may take it as quietly as possible, see that the shed is entirely free from dogs, chickens, or anything that would annoy him; then give him a few ears of corn, let him remain alone fifteen or twenty minutes, until he has examined his apartment, and has become reconciled to his confinement.

Time to Reflect.

And now, while your colt is eating those few ears of corn, is the proper time to see that your halter is ready and all right, and to reflect on the best mode of operations; for, in the horse-breaking, it is highly important that you should be governed by some system. And you should know, before you attempt to do anything, just what you are going to do, and how you are going to do it. And, if you are experienced in the art of taming wild horses, you ought to be able to tell, within a few minutes, the length of time it would take you to halter the colt, and teach him to lead.

The Kind of Halter.

Always use a leather halter, and be sure to have it made so that it will not draw tight around his nose if he pulls on it. It should be of the right size to fit his head easily and nicely; so that the nose band will not be too tight or too low. Never put a rope halter on an unbroken colt under any circumstances whatever. They have caused more horses to hurt or kill themselves, than would pay for twice the cost of all the leather halters that have ever been needed for the purpose of haltering colts. It is almost impossible to break a colt that is very wild with a rope halter, without having him pull, rear, and throw himself, and thus endanger his life; and I will tell you why. It is just as natural for a horse to try to get his head out of anything that hurts it or feels unpleasant, as it would be for you to try to get your hand out of a fire. The cords of the rope are hard and cutting; this makes him raise his head and draw on it, and, as soon as he pulls, the slip noose (the way rope halters are always made) tightens, and pinches his nose, and then he will struggle for life, until, perchance, he throws himself; and who would have his horse throw himself, and run the risk of breaking his neck, rather than pay the price of a leather halter. But this is not the worst. A horse that has once pulled on his halter, can never be as well broke as one that has never pulled at all.

Remarks on the Horse.

But before we attempt to do anything more with the colt, I will give you some of the characteristics of his nature, that you may better understand his motions. Every one that has ever paid any attention to the horse, has noticed his natural inclination to smell of everything which to him looks new and frightful. This is their strange mode of examining everything. And, when they are frightened at anything, though they look at it sharply, they seem to have no confidence in this optical examination alone, but must touch it with the nose before they are entirely satisfied; and, as soon as this is done, all is right.

Experiments with the Robe.

If you want to satisfy yourself of this characteristic of the horse, and learn something of importance concerning the peculiarities of his nature, etc., turn him into the barn-yard, or a large stable will do, and then gather up something that you know will frighten him; a red blanket, a buffalo robe, or something of that kind. Hold it up so that he can see it; he will stick up his head and snort. Then throw it down somewhere in the center of the lot or barn, and walk off to one side. Watch his motions, and study his nature. If he is frightened at the object, he will not rest until he has touched it with his nose. You will see him begin to walk around the robe and snort, all the time getting a little closer, as if drawn up by some magic spell, until he finally gets within reach of it. He will then very cautiously stretch out his neck as far as he can reach, merely touching it with his nose, as though he thought it was ready to fly at him. But after he has repeated these touches a few times, for the first (though he has been looking at it all the time) he seems to have an idea what it is. But now he has found, by the sense of feeling, that it is nothing that will do him any harm, and he is ready to play with it. And if you watch him closely, you will see him take hold of it with his teeth, and raise it up and pull at it. And, in a few minutes, you can see that he has not that same wild look about his eye, but stands like a horse biting at some familiar stump.

Yet the horse is never as well satisfied when he is about anything that has frightened him, as when he is standing with his nose to it. And, in nine cases out of ten, you will see some of that same wild look about him again, as he turns to walk from it. And you will, probably, see him looking back very suspiciously as he walks away, as though he thought it might come after him yet. And, in all probability, he will have to go back and make another examination before he is satisfied. But he will familiarize himself with it, and, if he should run into that lot a few days, the robe that frightened him so much at first, will be no more to him than a familiar stump.

Suppositions on the Sense of Smelling.

We might very naturally suppose, from the fact of the horse's applying his nose to everything new to him, that he always does so for the purpose of smelling these objects. But I believe that it is as much or more for the purpose of feeling; and that he makes use of his nose or muzzle, (as it is sometimes called,) as we would of our hands; because it is the only organ by which he can touch or feel anything with much susceptibility.

I believe that he invariably makes use of the four

senses, seeing, hearing, smelling, and feeling, in all of his examinations, of which the sense of feeling is, perhaps, the most important. And I think that in the experiment with the robe, his gradual approach and final touch with his nose, was as much for the purpose of feeling, as anything else, his sense of smell being so keen, that it would not be necessary for him to touch his nose against anything in order to get the proper scent; for it is said that a horse can smell a man the distance of a mile. And, if the scent of the robe was all that was necessary, he could get that several rods off. But, we know from experience, that if a horse sees and smells a robe a short distance from him, he is very much frightened, (unless he is used to it,) until he touches or feels it with his nose; which is a positive proof that feeling is the controlling sense in this case.

Prevailing Opinion of Horsemen.

It is a prevailing opinion among horsemen generally, that the sense of smell is the governing sense of the horse. And Foucher, as well as others, have, with that view, got up recipes of strong smelling oils, etc., to tame the horse, sometimes using the chestnut of his leg, which they dry, grind into powder, and blow into his nostrils; sometimes using the oil of rhodium, origanum, etc., that are noted for their strong smell; and sometimes they scent the hands with the sweat from under the arm, or blow their breath into his nostrils, etc. All of which, as far as the scent goes, have no effect whatever in gentling the horse, or conveying any idea to his mind; though the works that accompany these efforts—handling him, touching him about the nose and head, and patting him, as they direct you should, after administering the articles, may have a very great effect, which they mistake to be the ingredients used. And Faucher, in his work entitled, *The Arabian Art of Taming Horses,* page 17, tells us how to accustom a horse to a robe, by administering certain articles to his nose; and goes on to say, that these articles must first be applied to the horse's nose before you attempt to break him, in order to operate successfully.

Now, reader, can you, or any one else, give one single reason how scent can convey any idea to the horse's mind of what we want him to do? If not, then, of course, strong scents of any kind are of no account in taming the unbroken horse. For everything that we get him to do of his own accord, without force, must be accomplished by some means of conveying our ideas to his mind. I say to my horse, "Go 'long;" and he goes; "Ho!" and he stops; because these two words, of which he has learned the meaning by the tap of the whip, and the pull of the rein that first accompanied them, convey the two ideas to his mind of go and stop.

Faucher, or no one else, can ever teach the horse a single thing by the means of a scent alone.

How long do you suppose a horse would have to stand and smell of a bottle of oil before he would learn to bend his knee and make a bow at your bidding, "go yonder and bring your hat," or "come here and lay down?" Thus you see the absurdity of trying to break or tame the horse by means of recipes for articles to smell of, or medicine to give him, of any kind whatever.

The only science that has ever existed in the world, relative to the breaking of horses, that has been of any account, is that true method which takes them in their native state, and improves their intelligence.

Powel's System of Approaching the Colt.

But, before we go further, I will give you Willis J. Powel's system of approaching a wild colt, as given by him in a work published in Europe, about the year 1814, on the *Art of Taming Wild Horses.* He says: "A horse is gentled by my secret in from two to sixteen hours." The time I have most commonly employed has been from four to six hours. He goes on to say: "Cause your horse to be put in a small yard, stable, or room. If in a stable or room, it ought to be large, in order to give him some exercise with the halter before you lead him out. If the horse belongs to that class which appears only to fear man, you must introduce yourself gently into the stable, room, or yard where the horse is. He will naturally run from you; and frequently turn his head from you; but you must walk about extremely slow and softly, so that he can see you whenever he turns his head toward you, which he never fails to do in a short time, say in a quarter of an hour. I never knew one to be much longer without turning toward me.

"At the very moment he turns his head, hold out your left hand toward him, and stand perfectly still, keeping your eyes upon the horse, watching his motions, if he makes any. If the horse does not stir for ten or fifteen minutes, advance as slowly as possible, and without making the least noise, always holding out your left hand, without any other ingredient in it than that what nature put in it." He says: "I have made use of certain ingredients before people, such as the sweat under my arm, etc., to disguise the real secret, and many believed that the docility to which the horse arrived in so short a time, was owing to these ingredients; but you see, from this explanation, that they were of no use whatever. The implicit faith placed in these ingredients, though innocent of themselves, becomes 'faith without works.' And thus men remained always in doubt concerning this secret. If the horse makes the least motion when you advance toward him, stop, and remain perfectly still until he is quiet. Remain a few moments in this condition, and then advance again in the same slow and imperceptible manner. Take notice: if the horse stirs, stop without changing your position. It is very uncommon for the horse to stir more than once after you begin to advance, yet there are exceptions. He generally keeps his eyes steadfast on you, until you get near enough to touch him on the forehead. When you are thus near to him, raise slowly, and by degrees, your hand, and let it come in contact with that part just above the nostrils, as lightly as possible. If the horse flinches, (as many will,) repeat with great rapidity these light strokes upon the forehead, going a little further up toward his ears by degrees, and descending with the same rapidity, until he will let you handle his forehead all over. Now let the strokes be repeated with more force over all his forehead, descending by lighter strokes to each side of his head, until you can handle that part with equal facility. Then touch, in the same light manner, making your hands and fingers play around the lower part of the

4

horse's ears, coming down now and then to his forehead, which may be looked upon as the helm that governs all the rest.

"Having succeeded in handling his ears, advance toward the neck, with the same precautions, and in the same manner; observing always to augment the force of the strokes whenever the horse will permit it. Perform the same on both sides of the neck, until he lets you take it in your arms without flinching.

"Proceed in the same progressive manner to the sides, and then to the back of the horse. Every time the horse shows any nervousness, return immediately to the forehead, as the true standard, patting him with your hands, and from thence rapidly to where you had already arrived, always gaining ground a considerable distance further on every time this happens. The head, ears, neck, and body being thus gentled, proceed from the back to the root of the tail.

"This must be managed with dexterity, as a horse is never to be depended on that is skittish about the tail. Let your hand fall lightly and rapidly on that part next to the body a minute or two, and then you will begin to give it a slight pull upward every quarter of a minute. At the same time you continue this handling of him, augment the force of the strokes, as well as the raising of the tail, until you can raise it and handle it with the greatest ease, which commonly happens in a quarter of an hour in most horses; in others almost immediately, and in some much longer. It now remains to handle all his legs. From the tail come back again to the head, handle it well, as likewise the ears, breast, neck, etc., speaking now and then to the horse. Begin by degrees to descend to the legs, always ascending and descending, gaining ground every time you descend, until you get to his feet.

"Talk to the horse in Latin, Greek, French, English, or Spanish, or in any other language you please; but let him hear the sound of your voice, which, at the beginning of the operation, is not quite so necessary, but which I have always done in making him lift up his feet. Hold up your foot, 'Levez le pied,' 'Alza el pie,' 'Aron ton poda,' etc., at the same time lift his foot with your hand. He soon becomes familiar with the sounds, and will hold his foot up at command. Then proceed to the hind feet, and go on in the same manner, and in a short time the horse will let you lift them, and even take them up in your arms.

"All this operation is no magnetism, no galvanism; it is merely taking away the fear a horse generally has of a man, and familiarizing the animal with his master. As the horse doubtless experiences a certain pleasure from this handling, he will soon become gentle under it, and show a very marked attachment to his keeper."

Remarks on Powel's Treatment how to govern Horses of any Kind.

These instructions are very good, but not quite sufficient for horses of all kinds, and for haltering and leading the colt; but I have inserted it here, because it gives some of the true philosophy of approaching the horse, and of establishing confidence between man and horse. He speaks only of the kind that fear man.

To those who understand the philosophy of horsemanship, these are the easiest trained; for when we have a horse that is wild and lively, we can train him to our will in a very short time; for they are generally quick to learn, and always ready to obey. But there is another kind, that are of a stubborn or vicious disposition, and, although they are not wild, and do not require taming, in the sense it is generally understood, they are just as ignorant as a wild horse, if not more so, and need to be taught just as much; and, in order to have them obey quickly, it is very necessary that they should be made to fear their masters; for, in order to obtain perfect obedience from any horse, we must first have him fear us, for our motto is, *fear, love, and obey;* and we must have the fulfillment of the first two before we can expect the latter, and it is by our philosophy of creating fear, love and confidence, that we govern, to our will, every kind of a horse whatever.

Then, in order to take horses as we find them, or all kinds, and to train them to our likings, we will always take with us, when we go into a stable to train a colt, a long switch whip, (whale-bone buggy whips are the best,) with a good silk cracker, so as to cut keen and make a sharp report, which, if handled with dexterity, and rightly applied, accompanied with a sharp, fierce word, will be sufficient to enliven the spirits of any horse. With this whip in your right hand, with the lash pointing backward, enter the stable alone. It is a great disadvantage in training a horse, to have any one in the stable with you; you should be entirely alone, so as to have nothing but yourself to attract his attention. If he is wild you will soon see him in the opposite side of the stable from you; and now is the time to use a little judgment. I would not want for myself more than half or three-quarters of an hour to handle any kind of a colt, and have him running about in the stable after me; though I would advise a new beginner to take more time, and not be in too much of a hurry. If you have but one colt to gentle, and are not particular about the length of time you spend, and have not had any experience in handling colts, I would advise you to take Mr. Powel's method at first, till you gentle him, which he says takes from two to six hours. But, as I want to accomplish the same, and, what is much more, teach the horse to lead in less than one hour, I shall give you a much quicker process of accomplishing the same end. Accordingly, when you have entered the stable, stand still and let your horse look at you a minute or two, and as soon as he is settled in one place, approach him slowly, with both arms stationary, your right hanging by your side, holding the whip as directed, and the left bent at the elbow, with your hand projecting. As you approach him, go not too much toward his head or croop, so as not to make him move either forward or backward, thus keeping your horse stationary; if he does move a little forward or backward, step a little to the right or left very cautiously; this will keep him in one place; as you get very near him, draw a little to his shoulder, and stop a few seconds. If you are in his reach he will turn his head and smell at your hand, not that he has any preference for your hand, but because that it is projecting, and is the nearest portion of your body to the horse. This all colts will do, and they will smell of your naked hand just as quick as they will of anything that you can put in it, and with just as good an effect, however much some men have preached the doctrine of taming horses by giving them the scent articles from the hand. I have already proved that to be a mistake. As soon as he touches his nose to your hand, caress him as before directed, always using a very light, soft hand, merely touching the horse, always rubbing the way the hair lays, so that your hand will pass along as smoothly as possible. As you stand by his side you may find it more convenient to rub his neck or the side of his head, which will answer the same purpose as rubbing his forehead. Favor every inclination of the horse to smell or touch you with his nose. Always follow each touch or communication of this kind with the most tender and affectionate caresses, accompanied with a kind look. and pleasant word of some sort, such as: Ho! my little boy, ho! my little boy, pretty boy, nice lady! or something of that kind, constantly repeating the same words, with the same kind, steady tone of voice; for the horse soon learns to read the expression of the face and voice, and will know as well when fear, love, or anger, prevails as you know your own feelings; two of which, *fear and anger*, a good horseman *should never feel.*

How to proceed if your Horse is of a Stubborn Disposition.

If your horse, instead of being wild, seems to be of a stubborn or *mulish* disposition; if he lays back his ears as you approach him, or turns his heels to kick you, he has not that regard or fear of man that he should have, to enable you to handle him quickly and easily; and it might be well to give him a few sharp cuts with the whip, about the legs, pretty close to the body. It will crack keen as it plies around his legs, and the crack of the whip will affect him as much as the stroke; besides, one sharp cut about his legs will affect him more than two or three over his back, the skin on the inner part of his legs, or about his flank being thinner and more tender than on his back. But do not whip him much, just enough to scare him; it is not because we want to hurt the horse that we whip him; we only do it to scare that bad disposition out of him. But whatever you do, do quickly, sharply, and with a good deal of fire, but always without anger. If you are going to scare him at all you must do it at once. Never go into a pitched battle with your horse, and whip him till he is mad and will fight you; you had better not touch him at all, for you will establish, instead of fear and regard, feelings of resentment, hatred, and ill-will. It will do him no good, but an injury, to strike a blow, unless you can scare him; but if you succeed in scaring him, you can whip him without making him mad; for fear and anger never exist together in the horse, and as soon as one is visible, you will find that the other has disappeared. As soon as you have frightened him so that he will stand up straight and pay some attention to you, approach him again and caress him a good deal more than you whipped him; then you will excite the two controlling passions of his nature, love and fear, and then he will fear and love you too, and as soon as he learns what to do, will quickly obey.

How to halter and lead the Colt.

As soon as you have gentled the colt a little, take the halter in your left hand and approach him as before, and on the same side that you have gentled him. If he is very timid about your approaching closely to him, you can get up to him quicker by making the whip a part of your arm, and reaching out very gently with

the butt end of it, rubbing him lightly on the neck, all
the time getting a little closer, shortening the whip by
taking it up in your hand, until you finally get close
enough to put your hands on him. If he is inclined to
hold his head from you, put the end of the halter strap
around his neck, drop your whip, and draw very gently;
he will let his neck give, and you can pull his head to
you. Then take hold of that part of the halter which
buckles over the top of his head, and pass the long side,
or that part which goes into the buckle, under his neck,
grasping it on the opposite side with your right hand,
letting the first strap loose, the latter will be sufficient
to hold his head to you. Lower the halter a little, just
enough to get his nose into that part which goes around
it, then raise it somewhat, and fasten the top buckle,
and you will have it all right. The first time you halter
a colt you should stand on the left side, pretty well back
to his shoulder, only taking hold of that part of the halter that goes around his neck, then, with your hands
about his neck, you can hold his head to you, and raise
the halter on it without making him dodge by putting
your hands about his nose. You should have a long
rope or strap ready, and as soon as you have the halter
on, attach this to it, so that you can let him walk the
length of the stable without letting go of the strap, or
without making him pull on the halter, for if you only
let him feel the weight of your hand on the halter, and
give him rope when he runs from you, he will never
rear, pull, or throw himself, yet you will be holding
him all the time, and doing more toward gentling him
than if you had the power to snub him right up, and
hold him to one spot; because he does not know anything about his strength, and if you don't do anything

to make him pull, he will never know that he can. In a few minutes you can begin to control him with the halter, then shorten the distance between yourself and the horse, by taking up the strap in your hand.

As soon as he will allow you to hold him by a tolerably short strap, and step up to him without flying back, you can begin to give him some idea about leading. But to do this, do not go before and attempt to pull him after you, but commence by pulling him very quietly to one side. He has nothing to brace either side of his neck, and will soon yield to a steady, gradual pull of the halter; and, as soon as you have pulled him a step or two to one side, step up to him and caress him, and then pull him again, repeating this operation until you can pull him around in every direction, and walk about the stable with him, which you can do in a few minutes, for he will soon think, when you have made him step to the right or left a few times, that he is compelled to follow the pull of the halter, not knowing that he has the power to resist your pulling; besides, you have handled him so gently, that he is not afraid of you, and you always caress him when he comes up to you, and he likes that, and would just as leave follow you as not. And after he has had a few lessons of that kind, if you turn him out in a lot he will come up to you every opportunity he gets. You should lead him about in the stable some time before you take him out, opening the door, so that he can see out, leading him up to it and back again, and past it. See that there is nothing on the outside to make him jump, when you take him out, and as you go out with him, try to make him go very slowly, catching hold of the halter close to the jaw, with your left hand, while the right is resting on the top of the neck, holding to his mane. After you are out with him a little while, you can lead him about as you please. Don't let any second person come up to you when you first take him out; a stranger taking hold of the halter would frighten him, and make him run. There should not even be any one standing near him to attract his attention, or scare him. If you are alone, and manage him right, it will not require any more force to lead or hold him than it would to manage a broken horse.

How to lead a Colt by the Side of a broken Horse.

If you should want to lead your colt by the side of another horse, as is often the case, I would advise you to take your horse into the stable, attach a second strap to the colt's halter, and lead your horse up alongside of him. Then get on the broken horse and take one strap around his breast, under his martingale, (if he has any on,) holding it in your left hand. This will prevent the colt from getting back too far; besides, you will have more power to hold him, with the strap pulling against the horse's breast. The other strap take up in your right hand to prevent him from running ahead; then turn him about a few times in the stable, and if the door is wide enough, ride out with him in that position; if not, take the broken horse out first, and stand his breast up against the door, then lead the colt to the same spot, and take the straps as before directed, one on each side of his neck, then let some one start the colt out, and as he comes out, turn your horse to the left, and you will have them all right. This is the best way to lead a colt; you can manage any kind of a colt in this way, without any trouble; for, if he tries to run ahead, or pull back, the two straps will bring the horses facing each other, so that you can easily follow up his movements without doing much holding, and as soon as he stops running backward you are right with him, and all ready to go ahead. And if he gets stubborn and does not want to go, you can remove all his stubbornness by riding your horse against his neck, thus compelling him to turn to the right, and as soon as you have turned him about a few times, he will be willing to go along. The next thing, after you are through leading him, will be to take him into a stable, and hitch him in such a way as not to have him pull on the halter, and as they are often troublesome to get into a stable the first few times, I will give you some instructions about getting him in.

How to lead a Colt into the Stable and hitch him without having him pull on the Halter.

You should lead the broken horse into the stable first, and get the colt, if you can, to follow in after him. If he refuses to go, step up to him, taking a little stick or switch in your right hand; then take hold of the halter close to his head with your left hand, at the same time reaching over his back with your right arm, so that you can tap him on the opposite side with your switch; bring him up facing the door, tap him lightly with your switch, reaching as far back with it as you can. This tapping, by being pretty well back, and on the opposite side, will drive him ahead, and keep him close to you; then, by giving him the right direction with your left hand, you can walk into the stable with him. I have walked colts into the stable this way, in less than a minute, after men had worked at them half an hour, trying to pull them in. If you can not walk him in at once this way, turn him about and walk him round in every direction, until you can get him up to the door without pulling at him. Then let him stand a few minutes, keeping his head in, the right direction with the halter, and he will walk in in less than ten minutes. Never attempt to pull the colt into the stable; that would make him think at once that it was a dangerous place, and if he was not afraid of it before, he would be then. Besides, we don't want him to know anything about pulling on the halter. Colts are often hurt, and sometimes killed, by trying to force them into the stable; and those who attempt to do it in that way, go into an up-hill business, when a plain, smooth road is before them.

If you want to hitch your colt, put him in a tolerably wide stall, which should not be too long, and should be connected by a bar, or something of that kind to the partition behind it; so that, after the colt is in he can not get far enough back to take a straight, backward pull on the halter; then, by hitching him in the center of the stall, it would be impossible for him to pull on the halter, the partition behind preventing him from going back, and the halter in the center checking him every time he turns to the left or right. In a state of this kind you can break every horse to stand hitched by a light strap, anywhere, without his ever knowing anything about pulling. But if you have broken your horse to lead, and have taught him the use of the halter, (which you should always do before you hitch him to anything,) you can hitch him in any kind of a stall, and give him something to eat to keep him up to his place for a few minutes at first, and there is not one colt in fifty that will pull on his halter.

The kind of Bit and how to accustom a Horse to it.

You should use a large, smooth, snaffle bit, so as not to hurt his mouth, with a bar to each side, to prevent the bit from pulling through either way. This you should attach to the head-stall of your bridle, and put it on your colt without any reins to it, and let him run loose in a large stable or shed some time, until he becomes a little used to the bit, and will bear it without trying to get it out of his mouth. It would be well, if convenient, to repeat this several times before you do anything more with the colt; as soon as he will bear the bit, attach a single rein to it, without any martingal. You should also have a halter on your colt, or a bridle made after the fashion of a halter, with a strap to it, so that you can hold or lead him without pulling on the bit much. He is now ready for the saddle.

How to saddle a Colt.

Any one man, who has this theory, can put a saddle on the wildest colt that ever grew, without any help, and without scaring him. The first thing will be to tie each stirrup strap into a loose knot, to make them short, and prevent the stirrups from flying about and hitting him. Then, double up the skirts and take the saddle under your right arm, so as not to frighten him with it as you approach. When you get to him, rub him gently a few times with your hand, and then raise the saddle very slowly, until he can see it, and smell and feel it with his nose. Then let the skirts loose, and rub it very gently against his neck the way the hair lays, letting him hear the rattle of the skirts as he feels them against him; each time getting a little further backward, and finally slip it over his shoulders on his back. Shake it a little with your hand, and in less than five minutes you can rattle it about over his back as much as you please, and pull it off and throw it on again, without his paying much attention to it.

As soon as you have accustomed him to the saddle, fasten the girth. Be careful how you do this. It often frightens a colt when he feels the girth binding him, and making the saddle fit tight on his back. You should bring up the girth very gently, and not draw it too tight at first; just enough to hold the saddle on. Move him a little, and then girth it as tight as you choose, and he will not mind it.

You should see that the pad of your saddle is all right before you put it on, and that there is nothing to make it hurt him, or feel unpleasant to his back. It should not have any loose straps on the back part of it, to flap about and scare him. After you have saddled him in this way, take a switch in your right hand to tap him up with, and walk about in the stable a few times, with your right arm over the saddle, taking hold of the reins on each side of his neck, with your right and left hands, thus marching him about in the stable until you learn him the use of the bridle, and can turn him about in any direction, and stop him by a gentle pull of the rein. Always caress him, and loose the reins a little every time you stop him.

You should always be alone, and have your colt in some tight stable or shed the first time you ride him; the loft should be high, so that you can sit on his back without endangering your head. You can learn him more in two hours' time, in a stable of this kind, than you could in two weeks, in the common way of breaking colts, out in an open place. If you follow my course of treatment, you need not run any risk or have any trouble in riding the worst kind of a horse. You take him a step at a time, until you get up a mutual confidence and trust between yourself and horse. First learn him to lead and stand hitched, next acquaint him with the saddle and the use of the bit, and then all that remains, is to get on him without scaring him, and you can ride him as well as any horse.

How to mount the Colt.

First, gentle him well on both sides, about the saddle, and all over, until he will stand still without holding, and is not afraid to see you anywhere about him.

As soon as you have him thus gentled, get a small block, about one foot or eighteen inches in hight, and set it down by the side of him, about where you want to stand to mount him: step up on this, raising yourself very gently; horses notice every change of position very closely, and if you were to step up suddenly on the block, it would be very apt to scare him; but by raising yourself gradually on it, he will see you without being frightened, in a position very near the same as while you are on his back.

As soon as he will bear this without alarm, untie the stirrup strap next to you, and put your left foot into the stirrup, and stand square over it, holding your knee against the horse, and your toe out, so as to touch him under the shoulder with the toe of your boot. Place your right hand on the front of the saddle and on the opposite side of you, taking hold of a portion of the mane and the reins, as they hang loosely over his neck, with your left hand; then gradually bear your weight on the stirrup, and on your right hand, until the horse feels your whole weight on the saddle; repeat this several times, each time raising yourself a little higher from the block, until he will allow you to raise your leg over his croup, and place yourself in the saddle.

There are three great advantages in having a block to mount from. First, a sudden change of position is very apt to frighten a young horse that has never been handled; he will allow you to walk up to him and stand by his side without scaring at you, because you have gentled him to that position; but if you get down on your hands and knees, and crawl toward him, he will be very much frightened, and, upon the same principle, he would frighten at your new position, if you had the power to hold yourself over his back without touching him. Then the first great advantage of the block is to gradually gentle him to that new position in which he will see you when you ride him.

Secondly, by the process of leaning your weight in the stirrups, and on your hand, you can gradually accustom him to your weight, so as not to frighten him by having him feel it all at once. And, in the third place, the block elevates you so that you will not have to make a spring in order to get on to the horse's back, but from it you can gradually raise yourself into the saddle. When you take these precautions, there is no horse so wild but what you can mount him without making him jump. I have tried it on the worst horses that could be found, and have never failed in any case. When mounting, your horse should always stand without being held. A horse is never well broke when he has to be held with a tight rein while mounting; and a colt is never so safe to mount, as when you see that assurance of confidence, and absence of fear, which causes him to stand without holding.

How to ride a Colt.

When you want him to start do not touch him on the side with your heel, or do anything to frighten him and make him jump, but speak to him kindly, and if he does not start, pull him a little to the left until he starts, and then let him walk off slowly, with the reins loose. Walk him around in the stable a few times, until he gets used to the bit, and you can turn him about in every direction, and stop him as you please. It would be well to get on and off a good many times, until he gets perfectly used to it, before you take him out of the stable.

After you have trained him in this way, which should not take you more than one or two hours, you can ride him anywhere you choose, without ever having him jump or make any effort to throw you.

When you first take him out of the stable, be very gentle with him, as he will feel a little more at liberty to jump or run, and be a little easier frightened than he was while in the stable. But after handling him so much in the stable, he will be pretty well broke, and you will be able to manage him without trouble or danger.

When you first mount him, take a little the shortest hold on the left rein, so that if anything frightens him you can prevent him jumping by pulling his head around to you. This operation of pulling a horse's head around against his side will prevent any horse from jumping ahead, rearing up, or running away. If he is stubborn and will not go, you can make him move by pulling his head around to one side, when whipping would have no effect. And turning him around a few times will make him dizzy, and then, by letting him have his head straight, and giving him a little touch with the whip, he will go along without any trouble.

Never use martingals on a colt when you first ride him; every movement of the hand should go right to the bit in the direction in which it is applied to the reins, without a martingal to change the direction of the force applied. You can guide the colt much better without them, and learn him the use of the bit in much less time. Besides, martingals would prevent you from pulling his head around if he should try to jump.

After your colt has been rode until he is gentle and well accustomed to the bit, you may find it an advantage, if he carries his head too high, or his nose too far out, to put martingals on him.

You should be careful not to ride your colt so far at first as to heat, worry, or tire him. Get off as soon as you see he is a little fatigued; gentle him, and let him rest. This will make him kind to you, and prevent him from getting stubborn or mad.

The proper way to Bit a Colt.

Farmers often put bitting harness on a colt the first thing they do to him, buckling up the bitting as tight as they can draw it, to make him carry his head high, and then turn him out in a lot to run a half day at a time. This is one of the worst punishments that they could inflict on the colt, and very injurious to a young horse that has been used to running in pasture with his head down. I have seen colts so injured in this way that they never got over it.

A horse should be well accustomed to the bit before you put on the bitting harness, and when you first bit him you should only rein his head up to that point where he naturally holds it, let that be high or low; he will soon learn that he can not lower his head, and that raising it a little will loosen the bit in his mouth. This will give him the idea of raising his head to loosen the bit, and then you can draw the bitting a little tighter every time you put it on, and he will still raise his head to loosen it; by this means you will gradually get his head and neck in the position you want him to carry it, and give him a nice and graceful carriage without hurting him, making him mad, or causing his mouth to get sore.

If you put the bitting on very tight the first time, he can not raise his head enough to loosen it, but will bear on it all the time, and paw, sweat, and throw himself. Many horses have been killed by falling backward with the bitting on; their heads, being drawn up, strike the ground with the whole weight of the body. Horses that have their heads drawn up tightly should not have the bitting on more than fifteen or twenty minutes at a time.

How to drive a Horse that is very wild and has any vicious habits.

Take up one fore foot and bend his knee till his hoof is bottom upwards, and merely touching his body then slip a loop over his knee, and up until it comes above the pasture joint, to keep it up, being careful to draw the loop together between the hoof and pasture joint with a second strap of some kind, to prevent the loop from slipping down and coming off. This will leave the horse standing on three legs; you can now handle him as you wish, for it is impossible for him to kick in this position. There is something in this operation of taking up one foot that conquers a horse quicker and better than anything else you can do to him. There is no process in the world equal to it to break a kicking horse, for several reasons. First, there is a principle of this kind in the nature of the horse; that by conquering one member you conquer, to a great extent, the whole horse.

You have, perhaps, seen men operate upon this principle by sewing a horse's ears together, to prevent him from kicking. I once saw a plan given in a newspaper to make a bad horse stand to be shod, which was to fasten down one ear. There were no reasons given why you should do so; but I tried it several times, and thought it had a good effect—though I would not recommend its use, especially stitching his ears together. The only benefit arising from this process is, by disarranging his ears we draw his attention to them, and he is not so apt to resist the shoeing. By tying up one foot we operate, on the same principle, to a much better effect. When you first fasten up a horse's foot, he will sometimes get very mad, and strike with his knee, and try every possible way to get it down; but he cannot do that, and will soon give it up.

This will conquer him better than anything you could do, and without any possible danger of hurting himself, or you either, for you can tie up his foot and sit down and look at him until he gives up. When you find that he is conquered, go to him, let down his foot, rub his leg with your hand, caress him, and let him rest a little, then put it up again. Repeat this a few times, always putting up the same foot, and he will soon learn to travel on three legs, so that you can drive him some distance. As soon as he gets a little used to this way of traveling, put on your harness and hitch him to a sulky. If he is the worst kicking horse that ever raised a foot, you need not be fearful of his doing any damage while he has one foot up, for he can not kick, neither can he run fast enough to do any harm. And if he is the wildest horse that ever had harness on, and has run away every time he has been hitched, you can now hitch him in a sulky and drive him as you please. And, if he wants to run, you can let him have the lines, and the whip too, with perfect safety, for he can not go but a slow gait on three legs, and will soon be tired and willing to stop; only hold him enough to guide him in the right direction, and he will soon be tired and willing to stop at the word. Thus you will effectually cure him at once of any further notion of running off. Kicking horses have always been the dread of everybody; you always hear men say, when they speak about a bad horse, "I do n't care what he does, so he don't kick." This new method is an effectual cure for this worst of all habits. There are plenty of ways by which you can hitch a kicking horse and force him to go, though he kicks all the time; but this don't have any good effect toward breaking him, for we know that horses kick because they are afraid of what is behind them, and when they kick against it, and it hurts them, they will only kick the harder, and this will hurt them still more, and make them remember the scrape much longer, and make it more difficult to persuade them to have any confidence in anything dragging behind them ever after.

But by this new method you can hitch them to a rattling sulky, plow, wagon, or anything else in its worst shape. They may be frightened at first, but can not kick or do anything to hurt themselves, and will soon find that you do not intend to hurt them, and then they will not care anything more about it. You can then let down the leg and drive along gently without any further trouble. By this new process a bad kicking horse can be learned to go gentle in harness in a few hours' time.

Further remarks on Balking.

Horses know nothing about balking, only as they are brought into it by improper management, and when a horse balks in harness it is generally from some mismanagement, excitement, confusion, or from not knowing how to pull, but seldom from any unwillingness to perform all that he understands. High-spirited, free-going horses are the most subject to balking, and only so because drivers do not properly understand how to manage this kind. A free horse in a team may be so anxious to go, that when he hears the word he will start with a jump, which will not move the load, but give him such a severe jerk on the shoulders that he will fly back and stop the other horse; the teamster will continue his driving without any cessation, and by the time he has the slow horse started again he will find that the free horse has made another jump, and again flew back, and now he has them both baldly balked, and so confused that neither of them know what is the matter, or how to start the load. Next will come the slashing and cracking of the whip, and hallooing of the driver, till something is broken, or he is through with his course of treatment. But what a mistake the driver commits by whipping his horse for this act. Reason and common sense should teach him that the horse was willing to go, but did not know how to start the load. And should he whip him for that? If so, he should whip him again for not knowing how to talk. A man that wants to act with any rationality or reason, should not fly into a passion, but should always think before he strikes. It takes a steady pressure against the collar to move a load, and you can not expect him to act with a steady, determined purpose, while you are whipping him. There is hardly one balking horse in five hundred that will pull true from whipping; it is only adding fuel to the fire, and will make them more liable to balk another time. You always see horses that have been balked a few times turn their heads and look back, as soon as they are a little frustrated. This is because they have been whipped, and are afraid of what is behind them. This is an invariable rule with balked horses, just as much as it is for them to look around at their sides when they have the bots; in either case, they are deserving of the same sympathy, and the same kind, rational treatment.

When your horse balks, or is a little excited, if he wants to start quickly, or looks around and don't want to go, there is something wrong, and needs kind treatment immediately. Caress him kindly, and if he does not understand at once what you want him to do, he will not be so much excited as to jump and break things, and do everything wrong through fear. As long as you are calm, and can keep down the excitement of the horse, there are ten chances to have him understand you, where there would not be one under harsh treatment, and then the little flare up would not carry with it any unfavorable recollection, and he would soon forget all about it, and learn to pull true. Almost every wrong act the horse commits is from mismanagement, fear, or excitement; one harsh word will so excite a nervous horse as to increase his pulse ten beats in a minute.

When we remember that we are dealing with dumb brutes, and reflect how difficult it must be for them to understand our motions, signs, and language, we should never get out of patience with them because they do not understand us, or wonder at their doing things wrong. With all our intellect, if we were placed in the horse's situation, it would be difficult for us to understand the driving of some foreigner, of foreign ways and foreign language. We should always recollect that our ways and language are just as foreign and unknown to the horse as any language in the world is to us, and should try to practice what we could understand, were we the horse, endeavoring, by some simple means, to work on his understanding rather than on the different parts of his body. All balked horses can be started true and steady in a few minutes time; they are all willing to pull as soon as they know how, and I never yet found a balked horse that I could not teach him to start his load in fifteen, and often less than three minutes time.

Almost any team, when first balked, will start kindly, if you let them stand five or ten minutes, as though there was nothing wrong, and then speak to them with a steady voice, and turn them a little to the right or left, so as to get them both in motion before they feel the pinch of the load. But if you want to start a team that you are not driving yourself, that has been balked, fooled, and whipped for some time, go to them and hang the lines on their hames, or fasten them to the wagon, so that they will be perfectly loose; make the driver and spectators (if there are any) stand off some distance to one side, so as not to attract the attention of the horses; unloose their check-reins, so that they can get their heads down, if they choose; let them stand a few minutes in this condition, until you can see that they are a little composed. While they are standing you should be about their heads, gentling them; it will make them a little more kind, and the spectators will think that you are doing something that they do not understand, and will not learn the secret. When you have them ready to start, stand before them, and as you seldom have but one balky horse in a team, get as near in front of him as you can, and if he is too fast for the other horse, let his nose come against your breast; this will keep him steady, for he will go slow rather than run on you; turn them gently to the right, without letting them pull on the traces, as far as the tongue will let them go; stop them with a kind word, gentle them a little, and then turn them back to the left, by the same process. You will have them under your control by this time, and as you turn them again to the right, steady them in the collar, and you can take them where you please.

There is a quicker process that will generally start a balky horse, but not so sure. Stand him a little ahead, so that his shoulders will be against the collar, and then take up one of his fore feet in your hand, and let the driver start them, and when the weight comes against his shoulders, he will try to step; then let him have his foot, and he will go right along. If you want to break a horse from balking that has long been in that habit, you ought to set apart a half day for that purpose. Put him by the side of some steady horse; have check lines on them; tie up all the traces and straps, so that there will be nothing to excite them; do not rein them up, but let them have their heads loose. Walk them about together for some time as slowly and lazily as possible; stop often, and go up to your balky horse and gentle him. Do not take any whip about him, or do anything to excite him, but keep him just as quiet as you can. He will soon learn to start off at the word, and stop whenever you tell him.

As soon as he performs right, hitch him in an empty wagon; have it stand in a favorable position for starting. It would be well to shorten the stay chain behind the steady horse, so that if it is necessary he can take the weight of the wagon the first time you start them. Do not drive but a few rods at first; watch your balky horse closely, and if you see that he is getting excited, stop him before he stops of his own accord, caress him a little, and start again. As soon as they go well, drive them over a small hill a few times, and then over a large one, occasionally adding a little load. This process will make any horse true to pull.

To break a Horse to Harness.

Take him in a tight stable, as you did to ride him; take the harness and go through the same process that you did with the saddle, until you get him familiar with them, so that you can put them on him and rattle them about without his caring for them. As soon as he will bear this, put on the lines, caress him as you draw them over him, and drive him about in the stable till he will bear them over his hips. The lines are a great aggravation to some colts, and often frighten them as much as if you were to raise a whip over them. As soon as he is familiar with the harness and line, take him out and put him by the side of a gentle horse, and go through the same process that you did with the balking horse. Always use a bridle without blinds when you are breaking a horse to harness.

How to hitch a Horse in a Sulky.

Lead him to and around it; let him look at it, touch it with his nose, and stand by it till he does not care for it; then pull the shafts a little to the left, and stand by your horse in front of the off-wheel. Let some one stand on the right side of the horse, and hold him by the bit, while you stand on the left side, facing the sulky. This will keep him straight. Run your left hand back and let it rest on his hip, and lay hold of the shafts with your right hand, bringing them up very gently to the left hand, which still remains stationary. Do not let anything but your arm touch his back, and as soon as you have the shafts square over him, let the person on the opposite side take hold of one of them and lower them very gently on the shaft bearers. Be very slow and deliberate about hitching; the longer time you take, the better, as a general thing. When you have the shafts placed, shake them slightly, so that he will feel them against each side. As soon as he will bear them without scaring, fasten your braces, etc., and start him along very slowly. Let one man lead the horse to keep him gentle, while the other gradually works back with the lines, till he can get behind and drive him. After you have driven him in this way a short distance, you can get into the sulky, and all will go right. It is very important to have your horse go gently when you first hitch him. After you have walked him awhile, there is not half so much danger of his scaring. Men do very wrong to jump up behind a horse to drive him as soon as they have him hitched. There are too many things for him to comprehend all at once. The shafts, the lines, the harness, and the rattling of the sulky, all tend to scare him, and he must be made familiar with them by degrees. If your horse is very wild, I would advise you to put up one foot the first time you drive him.

How to make a Horse stand without holding.

After you have him well broken to follow you, stand him in the center of the stable—begin at his head to caress him, gradually working backward. If he moves, give him a cut with the whip, and put him back in the same spot from which he started. If he stands, caress him as before, and continue gentling him in this way until you can get round him without making him move. Keep walking around him, increasing your pace, and only touch him occasionally. Enlarge your circle as you walk around, and if he then moves, give him another cut with the whip, and put him back to his place. If he stands, go to him frequently and caress him, and then walk around him again. Do not keep him in one position too long at a time, but make him come to you occasionally, and follow you round in the stable. Then stand him in another place, and proceed as before. You should not train your horse more than half an hour at a time.

PART II.

THE GENERAL MANAGEMENT OF THE HORSE.

Breeding Horses.

IMPORTANT and necessary as it is to secure the best possible condition, make, and character of both sire and dam, it is not sufficient to insure complete success. In a world where briars, weeds, and poisonous grasses grow spontaneously, and the fruits and grains which support life are grown only by laborious cultivation, eternal vigilance is the price of good life and ample sustenance. The first conditions being settled, leave no recess for slumbering. The mare needs constant care. She must be kept in good health and condition, must be fed with care, both as regards quantity and quality; must be sheltered from storms and bad weather, must have exercise and room for recreation, avoiding sudden, violent exertion; must be kept free from the noxious gases of foul and ill-ventilated stables; should be combed and rubbed frequently, and, in short, everything should be done which tends to cultivate and sustain that condition of life, strength, action, and spirit to be desired in the offspring. The forming animal derives no elements of its being from other source than the mother's system. During gestation, her vital fluid fills the fœtal veins, and if, from any depressing or exhausting influence, that blood is deficient in vitality, it can not supply that life and energy, that perfection of development to the new being, which a better condition would impart. Every influence affecting injuriously the mother's health vitiates the life fountain of the new being; hence the necessity and value of the utmost care and attention during the period of gestation.

All the attention requisite before foaling, is equally important afterward. In the one case, the fœtus derives its nourishment direct from the blood of the mother; in the next, the foal obtains its sustenance from the milk made from that blood, and it is not less important that the blood be healthy and pure to insure the proper quantity and quality of nutriment to the young animal. For this reason the mare should not be put to hard work soon after foaling, nor, indeed, to severe and constant toil during the time of suckling her young. She should be well fed, and allowed good pasturage, affording both food and room for exercise. An idea that half-starved and stunted colts make tough, hardy horses, has long existed among a portion of the farming community, and so opposed is it to all facts, so contrary to all the teachings of reason and philosophy, so absurd in itself, that its very existence is astonishing. When every tissue of the organization is made up from the nutriment taken into the system, and from that only, as every one knows, it is not easy to conceive how those tissues should be better formed if only half supplied with forming materials; yet such has been the idea. And, though a few good animals have been raised in this manner, it needs but a moment's thought to decide that they must have been much better if well cared for, and fully fed. Observation, it is thought, will convince any one that such horses are imperfectly developed, are more liable to the encroachments of disease, are wanting in action and spirit, and do not exhibit that symmetry and beauty of form characteristic of well-fed animals.

Youatt, who has written much and scientifically upon the economy of the horse, says:

"The breeder may depend upon it, that nothing is gained by starving the mother and stinting the foal at this time. It is the most important period of the life of the horse; and if, from false economy, his growth is arrested, his puny form and want of endurance will ever afterward testify to the error that has been committed."

There is no principle of greater importance than the liberal feeding of the foal during the time of his growth, and particularly at the time of weaning. Bruised oats and bran, or other nutritious and easily digestible articles, should form a part of his daily food; and the farmer may be assured that the money is well invested which is expended on the liberal nourishment of the growing colt. With liberal range, he should have good shelter from storms and the inclemencies of the weather. Too often, however, after weaning, he is left to struggle on as he can, and becoming poor and dispirited, may be seen shivering beside a fence, rheum running from his eyes, his rough, shaggy, dirty coat a habitation for vermin, and himself a sad specimen of poverty and misery. Not a great number of such cases may be found at this time compared with the past;

but there is far too much carelessness and inattention to young animals of all kinds. The dictates of humane feeling, and the demand of the owner's purse, when understood, will remedy the evil; and reform, in these matters, as in most others, will come from a knowledge of, and reasons for the better way. The agricultural wealth not yet developed, both vegetable and animal, may some day astonish the dull eyes of the present old fogyish portion of young America.

The Horse in the Stable.

If one would have a good horse on the road, he must take care of him in the stable. To the man who is fond of that noble animal, the horse, the stable is no mean place which is the *home* of his faithful servant. A part of the secret of the differences among horses may be found in the different ways they are treated in the stable.

This building need not have the embellishment of architecture, nor be made air-tight; but it should be comfortable—made to promote the comfort of its occupant. It should be well ventilated, by allowing a draught of fresh air constantly to pass through it, especially during the warmer months. Do not allow the air of the stable to be made offensive and unhealthy by the presence of ammonia escaping from the excrements. Keep the air in your stable as sweet as it is in your own house; for such is necessary for the health of a horse.

Plaster of Paris used freely about the stable, is quite desirable, both on the score of comfort and profit. It is cruel to foster a noble horse in a stable where the air is suffocating on account of noxious gases constantly generating and escaping for want of a few quarts of some absorbent.

The floor of the stall should not have much inclination, only enough to allow the water to pass off. The more level the surface on which a horse stables, the better.

It is said that "sprung knees" are occasioned partly by standing on steep floors in the stable. That such a floor is not pleasant for the horse, is clearly seen in the fact that when such a stall is wide, the horse will stand across his stall, in order to find the most level position.

Let the horse feel as *naturally* as possible in the stable. He has been furnished with a long neck in order that he may reach down to feed, as he does in the pasture, and not that he may reach up and pull out a small lock of hay from the rack. Give a horse a manger to feed out of, so that he can enjoy eating, and do not oblige him to steal his fodder from a rack, with narrow spaces, as though he did not deserve his keeping. It is thought that a horse will waste his hay if he is fed from a manger; but he will not, if he has good hay, given in proper quantities.

Air.

The breathing of pure air is necessary to the existence and the health of man and beast. It is comparatively lately that this has been admitted, even in the management of our best stables. They have been close, and hot, and foul, instead of airy, cool, and wholesome.

The stable should be as large, compared with the number of horses that it is destined to contain, as circumstances will allow.

The stable with a loft over it should never be less than twelve feet high, and proper ventilation should be secured, either by tubes carried through the roof, or by gratings close to the ceiling. These gratings or openings should be enlarged or contracted by means of a covering or shutter, so that spring, summer, and autumn, the stable may possess nearly the same temperature with the open air, and in winter a temperature of not more than ten degrees above that of the external atmosphere.

If the stable is close, the air will not only be hot, but foul. The breathing of every animal contaminates it; and, when in the course of the night, with every aperture stopped, it passes again and again through the lungs, the blood can not undergo its proper and healthy change; digestion will not be so perfectly performed, and all the functions of life are injured. Let the owner of a valuable horse think of his passing twenty or twenty-two out of the twenty-four hours in this debilitating atmosphere! Nature does wonders in enabling every animal to accommodate itself to the situation in which it is placed, and the horse that lives in the stable-oven suffers less from it than would scarcely be conceived possible; but he does not, and can not, possess the power and the hardihood which he would acquire under other circumstances.

Grooming.

Many persons go at this business as if they were rubbing the skin of the rhinoceros, instead of that of one of the most sensitive of the animal race. A comb with part of the teeth gone should never be used; and whatever be the condition of the comb, it should be handled carefully about the legs and head of the animal. If a horse is not thus handled, he will soon become restive, and perhaps acquire the pernicious habits of kicking or biting. Bad habits once being formed, the horse is declared vicious, and is proscribed, when it is really the hostler who is entitled to the epithet and the proscription.

If the horse is very tender, it is better to wash with warm water, and use only a soft brush.

Much need not be said of this to the agriculturist, since custom, and apparently without ill effect, has allotted so little of the comb and brush to the farmer's horse. The animal that is worked all day, and turned out at night, requires little more to be done to him than to have the dirt brushed off his limbs. Regular grooming, by rendering his skin more sensible to the alteration of temperature, and the inclemency of the weather, would be prejudicial. The horse that is altogether turned out, needs no grooming. The dandruff, or scurf, which accumulates at the roots of the hair, is a provision of nature to defend him from the wind and the cold.

It is to the stabled horse, highly fed, and little or irregularly worked, that grooming is of so much consequence. Good rubbing with the brush, or the curry-comb, open the pores of the skin, circulates the blood to the extremities of the body, produces free and healthy perspiration, and stands in the room of exercise. No horse will carry a fine coat without either unnatural heat or dressing. They both effect the same purpose; they both increase the insensible perspiration; but the first does it at the expense of health and strength, while the second, at the same time that it produces a glow on the skin, and a determination of blood to it, rouses all the energies of the frame. It would be well for the proprietor if he were to insist—and to see that his orders are really obeyed—that the fine coat in which he and his groom so much delight, is produced by honest rubbing and not by a heated stable and thick clothing, and most of all, not by stimulating or injurious spices. The horse should be regularly dressed every day, in addition to the grooming that is necessary after work.

Light.

This neglected branch of stable management is of far more consequence than is generally imagined; and it is particularly neglected by those for whom these treatises are principally designed. The farmer's stable is frequently destitute of any glazed window, and has only a shutter, which is raised in warm weather, and closed when the weather becomes cold. When the horse is in the stable only during a few hours in the day, this is not of so much consequence, nor of so much, probably, with regard to horses of slow work; but to carriage horses and hackneys, so far, at least, as the eyes are concerned, a dark stable is little less injurious than a foul and heated one. In order to illustrate this, reference may be made to the unpleasant feeling, and the impossibility of seeing distinctly, when a man suddenly emerges from a dark place into the full blaze of day. The sensation of mingled pain and giddiness is not soon forgotten; and some minutes pass before the eye can accommodate itself to the increased light. If this were to happen every day, or several times in the day, the sight would be irreparably injured, or possibly, blindness would ensue. Can we wonder, then, that the horse, taken from a dark stable into a glare of light, feeling, probably, as we should under similar circumstances, and unable for a considerable time to see anything around him distinctly, or that the frequently repeated violent effect of sudden light should cause inflammation of the eye so intense as to terminate in blindness? There is, indeed, no doubt that horses kept in dark stables are frequently notorious starters, and that abominable habit has been properly traced to this cause.

Exercise.

The first rule we would lay down is, that every horse should have daily exercise. The animal that, with the usual stable feeding, stands idle for three or four days, as is the case in many establishments, must suffer. He is predisposed to fever, or to grease, or, most of all, diseases of the foot; and if, after three or four days of inactivity, he is ridden far and fast, he is almost sure to have inflammation of the lungs or of the feet.

A gentleman's or a tradesman's horse suffers a great deal more from idleness than he does from work. A stable-fed horse should have two hours' exercise every day if he is to be kept free from disease. Nothing of extraordinary, or even of ordinary labor, can be effected on the road or in the field, without sufficient and regular exercise. It is this alone which can give energy to the system, or develop the powers of any animal.

Litter.

No heap of fermenting dung should be suffered to remain during the day in the corner, or in any part of the stable. With regard to this, the directions of the master should be peremptory.

The stable should be so contrived that the urine shall quickly run off, and the offensive and injurious vapor from the decomposing fluid and the litter will thus be materially lessened; but if this is effected by means of gutters and a descending floor, the descent must be barely sufficient to cause the fluid to escape, as, if the toes are kept higher than the heels, it will lead to lameness, and is also a frequent cause of contraction of the foot. Stalls of this kind certainly do best for mares; but for horses we much prefer those with a grating in the center, and a slight inclination of the floor on every side toward the middle. A short branch may communicate with a large drain, by means of which the urine may be carried off to a reservoir outside the stable. Traps are now contrived, and may be procured at little expense, by means of which neither any offensive smell nor current of air can pass through the grating.

Food.

There are few horses that do not habitually waste a portion of their hay; and, by some, the greater part is pulled down and trampled under foot, in order first to cull the sweetest and best locks, and which could not be done while the hay was inclosed in the rack. The observation of this induced the adoption of manger-feeding, or of mixing a portion of chaff (*i. e.*, cut feed) with the grain and beans. By this means the animal is compelled to chew his food; he can not, to any degree, waste the straw or hay; the chaff is too hard and too sharp to be swallowed without sufficient mastication, and, while he is forced to grind that down, the oats and beans are ground with it, and yield more nourishment; the stomach is more slowly filled, and therefore acts better on its contents, and is not so likely to be overloaded; and the increased quantity of saliva thrown out in the lengthened maceration of the food softens it, and makes it more fit for digestion.

Chaff may be composed of equal quantities of clover or meadow hay and wheaten, oaten, or barley straw, cut into pieces of a quarter or half an inch in length, and mingled well together; the allowance of oats or beans is afterward added, and mixed with the chaff.

For the agricultural and cart horse, eight pounds of oats and two of beans should be added to every twenty pounds of chaff. Thirty-four or thirty-six pounds of the mixture will be sufficient for any moderate sized horse, with fair, or even hard work. The dray or wagon horse may require forty pounds. Hay in the rack at night is, in this case, supposed to be omitted altogether. The rack, however, may remain, as occasionally useful for the sick horse, or to contain tares or other green feed. We would caution the farmer not to set apart too much damaged hay for the manufacture of the chaff. Much more injury is done by eating damaged hay or musty oats than is generally imagined.

There will be sufficient saving in the diminished cost of the provender, by the introduction of the straw and the improved condition of the horse, without poisoning him with the refuse of the farm. For old horses, and for those with defective teeth, chaff is peculiarly useful, and for them the grain should be broken down as well as the fodder.

While the mixture of chaff with the grain prevents it from being too rapidly devoured, and a portion of it swallowed whole, and therefore the stomach is not too loaded with that on which, as containing the most nutriment, its chief digestive power should be exerted, yet, on the whole, a great deal of time is gained by this mode of feeding, and more is left for rest. When a horse comes in wearied at the close of the day, it occupies, after he has eaten his grain, two or three hours to clear his rack. On the system of manger-feeding, the chaff being already cut into small pieces, and the beans and oats bruised, he is able fully to satisfy his appetite in an hour and a half. Two additional hours are, therefore, devoted to rest. This is a circumstance deserving of much consideration even in the farmer's stable, and of immense consequence to the post-rider, the stage-coach proprietor, and the owner of every hard-worked horse.

Manger food will be the usual support of the farmer's horse during the winter, and while at constant or occasional hard work; but from the middle of April to the end of July, he may be fed with this mixture in the day and turned out at night, or he may remain out during every rest day. A team in constant employ should not, however, be suffered to be out at night after the end of July.

The farmer should take care that the pasture is thick and good; and that the distance from the yard is not too great, or the fields too large, otherwise a very considerable portion of time will be occupied in catching the horse in the morning. He will likewise have to take into consideration the sale he would have for his hay, and the necessity for sweet and untrodden pasture for his cattle. On the whole, however, turning out in this way, when circumstances will admit of it, will be found to be more beneficial for the horse, and cheaper than soiling in the yard,

Few grooms make good gruel; it is either not boiled long enough, or a sufficient quantity of oatmeal has not been used. The proportions should be, a pound of meal thrown into a gallon of water, and kept constantly stirred until it boils, and five minutes afterward.

Barley is more nutritious than oats, containing nine hundred and twenty parts of nutritive matter in every thousand. There seems, however, to be something necessary beside a great proportion of nutritive matter in order to render any substance wholesome, strengthening, or fattening; therefore it is that, in many horses that are hardly worked, and, indeed, in horses generally, barley does not agree with them so well as oats. They are occasionally subject to inflammatory complaints, and particularly to surfeit and mange.

When barley is given, the quantity should not exceed a peck daily. It should always be bruised, and the chaff should consist of equal quantities of hay and barley-straw, and not cut too short.

Wheat contains nine hundred and fifty-five parts of nutritive matter. Wheat contains a greater portion of *gluten*, or sticky, adhesive matter, than any other kind of grain. It is difficult of digestion, and apt to cake and form obstructions in the bowels. This will oftener be the case if the horse is suffered to drink much water soon after feeding upon wheat. But a horse that is fed on wheat should have very little hay. The proportion should not be more than one truss of hay to two of straw.

Bran, or the ground husk of the wheat, used to be frequently given to benefit some sick horses, on account of the supposed advantage derived from its relaxing the bowels. There is no doubt that it does operate gently on the intestinal canal, and assists in quickening the passage of its contents, when it is occasionally given; but it must not be a constant, or even frequent food. Bran may, however, be useful as an occasional aperient in the form of a mash, but never should become a regular article of food.

Beans form a striking illustration of the principle that the nourishing or strengthening effects of the different articles of food depend more on some peculiar property which they possess, or some combination which they form, than on the actual quantity of nutritive matter. Beans contain but five hundred and seventy parts of nutritive matter, yet they add materially to the vigor of a horse. There are many horses that will not stand hard work without beans being mingled with their food, and these horses whose tendency to purge, it may be necessary to restrain, by the astringency of the bean. There is no traveler who is not aware of the difference in the spirit and continuance of his horse whether he allows or denies him beans on his journey. They afford not merely a temporary stimulus, but they may be daily used without losing their power, or producing exhaustion. They are indispensable to the hard-worked coach horse.

The straw of the bean is nutritive and wholesome, and is usually given to the horses. Its nutritive properties are supposed to be little inferior to those of oats. The small and plump bean is generally the best.

Peas appear to be, in a slight degree, more nourishing than beans, and not so heating. They contain five hundred and seventy-four parts of nutritive matter. For horses of slow work they may be used; but the quantity of chaff should be increased and a few oats added.

Linseed is sometimes given to sick horses—raw, ground, and boiled. It is supposed to be useful in cases of catarrh.

Hay is most in perfection when it is about a twelvemonth old. The horse would prefer it earlier, but it is neither so wholesome nor so nutritive, and often has a purgative quality. When it is about a year old, it retains, or should retain, somewhat of its green color, its agreeable smell, and its pleasant taste. It has undergone the slow process of fermentation, by which the sugar which it contains is developed, and its nutritive quality is fully exercised. Old hay becomes dry and tasteless, innutritive and unwholesome.

It is a good practice to sprinkle the hay with water in which salt has been dissolved. It is evidently more palatable to the animal, who will leave the best unsalted hay for that of an inferior quality that has been moistened with brine; and there can be no doubt that the salt very materially assists the progress of digestion. The preferable way of salting hay is to sprinkle it over the different layers as the rick is formed.

Of the value of tares, as forming a portion of the late spring and summer food of the stabled and agricultural horse, there can be no doubt. They are cut after the pods are formed, but a considerable time before the seeds are ripe. They supply a larger quantity of food for a limited time than almost any other forage crop. When surfeit-lumps appear on the skin, and the horse begins to rub himself against the divisions of the stall, and the legs swell, and the heels threaten to crack, a few tares, cut up with the chaff, or given instead of a portion of the hay, will afford considerable relief. Ten or twelve pounds may be allowed daily, and half that weight of hay subtracted.

Rye grass affords a valuable article of food, but it is inferior to the tare. It is not so nutritive. It is apt to scour, and occasionally, and late in the spring, it is injurious to the horse.

Clover is inferior to the tare and the rye grass, but nevertheless, is useful when they can not be obtained. Clover hay is, perhaps, preferable to meadow hay for chaff. It will sometimes tempt the sick horse, and may be given with advantage to those of slow and heavy work.

Carrots; this root is held in much esteem. There is none better, nor perhaps so good. When first given it is slightly diuretic and laxative; but as the horse becomes accustomed to it, these effects cease to be produced. They also improve the state of the skin. They form a good substitute for grass, and an excellent alterative for horses out of condition.

Potatoes have been given, and with advantage, in their raw state, sliced with the chaff; but, where it has been convenient to boil or steam them, the benefit has been far more evident. Purging has then rarely ensued. Half a dozen horses would soon repay the expense of a steaming boiler in the saving of provender, without taking into the account their improved condition and capability for work.

The times of feeding should be as equally divided as convenience will permit; and when it is likely that the horse will be kept longer than usual from home, the nose-bag should invariably be taken. The small stomach of the horse is emptied in a few hours, and if he is suffered to remain hungry much beyond his accustomed time, he will afterward devour his food so voraciously as to distend the stomach, and endanger an attack of staggers.

WATER.—This is a part of stable management little regarded by the farmer. There is nothing in which the different effect of hard and soft water is so evident, as in the stomach and digestive organs of the horse. Hard water, drawn fresh from the well, will assuredly make the coat of a horse unaccustomed to it stare, and it will not unfrequently gripe and otherwise injure him. He is injured, however, not so much by the hardness of the well-water as by its coldness—particularly by its coldness in summer, and when it is many degrees below the temperature of the atmosphere. The water in the brook and the pond being warmed by long exposure to the air, as well as having become soft, the horse drinks freely of it without danger.

There is a prejudice in the minds of many persons against the horse being fully supplied with water. They think that it injures his wind, and disables him for quick and hard work. If he is galloped, as he too often is, immediately after drinking, his wind may be too often irreparably injured; but if he were oftener suffered to satiate his thirst at the intervals of rest, he would be happier and better. It is a fact unsuspected by those who have not carefully observed the horse, that if he has frequent access to water, he will not drink so much in the course of the day as another will do, who, to cool his parched mouth, swallows as fast as he can, and knows not when to stop.

On a journey, a horse should be liberally supplied with water. When he is a little cooled, two or three quarts may be given to him, and after that his feed. Before he has finished his corn, two or three quarts more may be offered. He will take no harm if this is repeated three or four times during a long and hot day.

The Sense of Smell.

The sense of smell is so much used by the horse, that many have supposed he could be charmed by certain compounds of peculiar odor. Fancher and others used horse-chestnuts, origanum, rhodium, and various Oriental mixtures concocted by quacks, for the purpose of charming the horse.

No doubt anything that is pleasing to the sense of smell in the horse, will please him; and so far as you gratify this sense by the application of pleasing aromatics, so far you gain the confidence and favor of the horse, just as you would do by giving him a good dinner; but that there is anything about this sense in the horse that can be appealed to or made available by any unnatural or unphilosophical means, is as great a humbug as the celebrated "love powders" made into lozenges, which green ones are induced to purchase for the purpose of making some favorite lass love them against her will. Dismiss all such nonsense at once, and act upon the hypothesis that there is true philosophy in the mode of accomplishing anything.

The horse uses his nose, because he has not hands, as we have, to feel of objects; just as the elephant uses his trunk.

But this continual use of the nose in the horse is not to be overlooked or neglected. Since it is *his* mode of detecting the harmlessness or hurtfulness of any object, you must always submit everything to this test. If you know it is a mere whim in your horse, and a very unsuccessful way of detecting a steel trap from a coffee-mill, still it is *his* way, and you should always satisfy him by letting him smell of every object he desires to, except a steel trap or a pot of snuff.

Once his sense of smell tells him that a handkerchief, a halter, a stirrup, a bed-blanket, or anything else that attracts his notice and excites his fears, will not hurt him, he will then go to it, or allow you to put it on him. There need be no *superstitious* notions entertained in regard to it—it is enough if such results are produced by natural and philosophical principles.

Management of the Feet.

This is the only division of stable mangement that remains to be considered, and one sadly neglected by the carter and groom. The feet should be carefully examined every morning, for the shoes may be loose, and the horse would have been stopped in the middle of his work; or the clenchers may be raised, and endanger the wounding of his legs; for the shoe may begin to press upon the sole or the heel, and bruises of the sole, or corn, may be the result; and, the horse having stood so long in the stable, every little increase of heat in the foot, or lameness, will be more readily detected, and serious disease may often be prevented.

When the horse comes in at night, and after the harness has been taken off and stowed away, the heels should be well brushed out. Hand-rubbing will be preferable to washing, especially in the agricultural horse, whose heels, covered with long hair, can scarcely be dried again. If the dirt is suffered to accumulate in that long hair, the heels will become sore, and grease will follow; and if the heels are washed, and particularly during the winter, grease will result from the coldness occasioned by the slow evaporation of the moisture. The feet should be stopped—even the feet of the farmer's horse, if he remains in the stable. Very little clay should be used in the stopping, for it will get hard and press upon the sole. Cow-dung is the best stopping to preserve the feet cool and elastic; but before the stopping is applied, the picker should be run around the whole of the foot, between the shoe and the sole, in order to detect any stone that may have insinuated itself there, or a wound on any other part of the sole. For the hackney and hunter, stopping is indispensable. After several days' hard work it will afford very great relief to take the shoes off, having put plenty of litter under the horse, or to turn him, if possible, into a loose box; and the shoes of every horse, whether hardly worked or not, should be removed or changed once in every three weeks.

Points of a good Horse.

He should be about fifteen and a half hands high; the head light, and clean made; wide between the nostrils, and the nostrils themselves large, transparent, and open; broad in the forehead, eyes prominent, clear and sparkling; ears small, neatly set on; neck rather short, and well up; large arm or shoulder, well thrown back, and high; withers arched and high; legs fine, flat, thin, and small boned; body round and rather light, though sufficiently large to afford substance when it is needful; chest, affording play for the lungs; back short, the hind quarter set on rather obliquely. Any one possessing a horse of this make, and weighing eleven or twelve hundred pounds, may rest assured he is a horse of all work, and a bargain well worth getting hold of.

The Age of Horses after the Ninth year.

In relation to a new way of telling a horse's age, the *Southern Planter* says: "A few days ago we met a gentleman from Alabama, who gave us a piece of information in regard to ascertaining the age of a horse, after he or she has passed the ninth year, which was new to us, and will be, we are sure, to most of our readers. It is this: After the horse is nine years old, a wrinkle comes on the eyelid at the upper corner of the lower lid, and every year thereafter, he has one well-defined wrinkle for every year over nine. If, for instance, the horse has three wrinkles, he is twelve; if four, he is thirteen. Add the number of wrinkles to nine, and you will always get it. So says the gentleman; and he is confident it will never fail. A good many people have horses over nine; it is easily tried. If true, the horse dentist must give up his trade."

The Age of Horses by the Teeth.

A horse has six teeth above and six below in the fore mouth, which are called the cutting teeth. At two and a half years old it changes, two on top and two on the bottom, which are called the nippers; at three and a half years old, it changes two others called the separates; at four and a half, it changes the rook teeth; and at five years old he has a full mouth, when the tusks, or bridle-fangs, rise; at six years old the rook teeth are a little hollow, and at seven, there is a black mark, like the end of a ripe bean; at eight or nine the teeth wear smooth on the end again.

PART III.

DISEASES AND THEIR CURE.

To Mix and Give a Ball.

A BALL should never weigh more than an ounce and a half; it should be an inch in diameter, and two to three inches long. Lard is the best to mix your medicine in. Inclose in stout, soft paper. Back the horse in a stall, talk to him in a kindly tone, treat him gently; have the ball in the right hand, with the left gently draw out the tongue and hold it on the off-side of the mouth, pressing the fingers against the side of the lower jaw. Now, with the right hand pass the ball down the throat, not losing your hold of it, nor letting it touch the tongue or sides of the mouth until it reaches the palate; then give it a toss, instantly withdrawing the hand, and give the horse a slight tap under the chin, and down it will go.

Glanders.

When you think your horse has this disease, separate him from all other horses until you are sure. The best cure I know of is to kill the horse and burn the stable; or, at least, it might save others from taking the disease.

There should be much care taken to prevent this disease, as I have known men to take and die with it.

Diseases of the Teeth.

Of the diseases of the teeth in the horse, we know but little. Carious or hollow teeth are occasionally, but not often, seen; but the edges of the grinders, from the wearing off of the enamel, or the irregular growth of the teeth, become rough, and wound the inside of the cheek. It is then necessary to adopt a summary, but effectual mode of cure; namely, to rasp them smooth. Many bad ulcers have been produced in the mouth by neglect of this.

The teeth sometimes grow irregularly in length. They should be reduced to the level of the others with a saw, and occasionally looked to, because the difficulty will return. Decayed teeth should be removed, to prevent injury to the other teeth and to the jaw.

Fever, cough, catarrhal affections generally, disease of the eyes, cutaneous affections, diarrhea, loss of appetite, and general derangement, will frequently be traced by the careful observer to irritation from teething in the colt.

It is a rule scarcely admitting of the slightest deviation, that, when young horses are laboring under any febrile affection, the mouth should be examined, and, if the tushes are prominent, and pushing against the gums, a cut in the form of a cross should be made upon them. Relief will often be immediate.

Inflammation of the Eye.

Diseases of the eye in horses and mules, in this country, are very numerous. Names to this are like branches to a tree, almost from one common cause: cold, exposure, sweat, and dust. The best remedy I know of is, to take four ounces of golden seal, (hydrastine,) pour about six quarts of boiling water to it; when cool strain, and add four ounces of sulphurate of zinc, and one pint of laudanum; bathe the eye in the above wash often, getting as much as possible in the eye. If inflammation is very high, pack the head with sponges wet with cold water. Re-wet often.

The above I have tried for many years, on both man and beast, with great satisfaction and success.

Lung Fever.

This disease is but very little understood, or rather, not understood at all; the common way of treating it is to doctor the effect instead of removing the cause, which is *cold;* costiveness, inflammation, and fever being the effect. First give a ball, as follows:

Bayberry,	one ounce.
Cayenne,	half ounce.
Ginger,	one ounce.
Aloes,	one ounce.

The above is sufficient for two doses; repeat every four hours. Always give your horse warm water, with slippery elm bark, pulverized, and a little sweet spirits nitre in it, to drink. Water with the above often; keep your horse well wrapped in warm blankets; bear in mind to give injections often; use all the above articles steeped strong and sweetened well with molasses.

N. B.—Always guard against costiveness, in both man and beast; wrap the legs in poultices made of mustard and rye meal; change often, always washing with Castile soapsuds.

Distemper, how Cured.

Use the balls as in lung fever; also smoke the head and nostrils with tar and cotton.

Condition Powders.

One ounce of preventive being worth a pound of cure, I will give you a recipe for keeping your horse in good health; also, it may be used in slight cases of disease:

Antimony,	half pound.
Sulphur,	half pound.
Resin,	half pound.
Copperas.	quarter pound.
Aniseed,	half pound.
Saltpetre,	quarter pound.

Give a table-spoonful in his feed every third day.

To prevent the mane and tail from falling off, also to make them grow long and heavy:

Milk of sulphur,	two ounces.
Sugar of lead,	one ounce.
Rose water,	two quarts.

Bathe night and morning.

Heaves.

This malady is thought by many to be incurable; the reason why is, they do not know the cause. Heaves are caused by over-driving, taking cold, and inflammation, and dryness on the glands follows; not, as many suppose, a defect in the lungs. To cure, you should bathe and rub the part affected in some good liniment; also give the following powder:

Black pepper,	one pound.
Pleurisy root,	three ounces.
Aniseed,	three ounces.
Black antimony,	three ounces.
Cubebs,	three ounces.
Golden seal,	three ounces.

Pulverize and mix well together; give a table-spoonful in chop every morning; also sprinkle his hay with lime-water.

LINIMENT FOR THE HEAVES.

Alchohol,	one pint.
Spirits ammonia,	two ounces.
Camphor,	half ounce.
Gum myrrh,	half ounce.

After bathing with the above, grease the parts with olive oil.

String Halt.

This complaint is thought by some to run in the blood; by others to be a sudden contraction of the muscle, caused by a strain. I never knew a lazy, dull, sluggish horse or colt to have the string halt. I have known colts to bring it on by rearing, springing, slipping, or falling. Horses sometimes have it from turning corners suddenly, or from a desperate effort to start quick under the whip or spur. It does not injure a horse so much to be driven fast, after once started, as it does to be compelled to start quick, particularly if he is drawing a load. To cure, use liniment for strains and sprains, or liniment for heaves.

Caution.

Never start your horse suddenly, or by the use of the whip or spur. It not only injures the horse, but makes him restless and uneasy when you are getting upon his back, or into the carriage; it may endanger the lives of others, if not your own.

Poll Evil.

From the horse rubbing and sometimes striking his poll against the lower part of the manger, or hanging back in the stall and bruising the part with the halter, or from the frequent and painful stretching of the ligaments and muscles, by unnecessarily tight reining, and, occasionally, from a violent blow on the poll, inflammation ensues, and a swelling appears, hot, tender, and painful.

The best way to cure it is to take a small strap of leather, soak it in spirits of turpentine; take your needle and insert it; the needle should enter at the top of the tumor, penetrate through its bottom, and bring it out at the side of the neck, a little below the abscess. Wash often in warm water and castile soap, to keep clean, and prevent the hair from coming off.

Strangles.

This is a disease principally incident to young horses. It is preceded by a cough, and can not, at first, be distinguished from common cough; however, it soon commences with a discharge from the nostrils, of a yellowish color, mixed with pus, and generally without smell.

Mix a ball of saltpetre,	one drachm.
Black antimony,	one drachm.
Sulphur,	one drachm.
Honey,	one ounce.

To be given every other day. Food light; keep warm and dry.

Bots

Are caused by the egg of the gad-fly being licked from the skin of the horse, and thus conveyed to the stomach, where they are hatched, cling to the stomach, and are, finally, evacuated.

Some writers contend they are incurable, while others recommend fresh blood, sweetened milk, or anything that will nauseate slightly. A writer in the *Eastern Agriculturist* recommends giving a few sheaves of barley.

I use one pint of molasses and one pint of sweet milk, with the addition of half an ounce of alum, and the same bulk of charcoal, pulverized, well shook together; pour it down the neck of the horse; as soon as you think the bots have filled themselves, follow with one half pint of sweet spirits nitre, and the same quantity of linseed oil, which will soon pass them off; then give a ball of mustard-seed pulverized.

Tetanus or Lock-Jaw.

The horse, for a day or two, does not appear to be quite well; he does not feed as usual; he partly chews his food, and drops it; and he gulps his water. The ears are erect, pointed forward, and immovable; if the horse is spoken too, or threatened to be struck, they change not their position. The treatment of tetanus is simple. Take

Opium,	half drachm.
Copperas,	half drachm.
Aloes	four drachms.

Give, in the form of a ball, for three successive evenings.

Mange

Is a pimpled or vesicular eruption. After a while the vesicles break, or the cuticle and the hair fall off, and there is, as in obstinate surfeit, a bare spot covered with scurf—some fluid oozing from the skin beneath, and this changing to a scab, which likewise soon peels off, and leaves a wider spot. This process is attended with considerable itching and tenderness, and thickening of the skin, which soon becomes more or less folded, or puckered. The mange generally first appears on the neck, at the root of the mane, and its existence may be suspected even before the blotches appear, and when there is only considerable itchiness of the part, by the ease with which the short hair at the root of the mane is plucked out. From the neck it spreads upward to the head, or downward to the withers and back, and occasionally extends over the whole carcass of the horse.

One cause of it is neglected or inveterate surfeit. Several instances are on record in which poverty of condition, and general neglect of cleanliness, preceded or produced the most violent mange. The most common cause is contagion. Amid the whole list of diseases to which the horse is exposed, there is not one more highly contagious than mange. If it once gets into a stable it spreads through it; for the slightest contact seems sufficient for the communication of this noisome complaint.

If the same brush and curry-comb is used on all the horses, the propagation of mange is assured; and horses feeding in the same pasture with a mangy one rarely escape, from the propensity they have to nibble one another.

The propriety of bleeding, in cases of mange, depends on the condition of the patient. If mange is the result of poverty, and the animal is much debilitated, bleeding will increase the evil, and will probably deprive the constitution of the power of rallying. Physic, however, is indispensable in every case. But mange in the horse resembles itch in the human being; medicine alone will never effect a cure. There must be some local application. Sulphur is indispensable for mange. In an early and not very acute state of mange, equal portions of sulphur, turpentine, and train-oil, gently but well rubbed on the part, will be applied with advantage. A tolerably stout brush, or even a curry-comb, lightly applied, should be used, in order to remove the dandruff or scurf. After that, the horse should be washed with strong soap and water, as far as the disease has extended; and, when he has been thoroughly dried, the ointment should be well rubbed in with the naked hand, or with a piece of flannel.

During the application of the ointment, and as soon as the physic has set, an alterative ball or powder should be daily given. If, after some days have passed, no progress should appear to have been made, half a pound of sulphur should be well mixed with a pint of oil of tar, or, if that is not to be obtained, a pint of

Barbadoes tar, and the affected parts rubbed as before. On every fifth or sixth day, the ointment should be washed off with warm soap and water. The progress toward cure will thus be ascertained, and the skin will be cleansed, and its pores opened for the more effectual application of the ointment.

It will be prudent to give two or three dressings after the horse has been apparently cured, and to continue the alteratives for ten days or a fortnight.

Surfeit.

Large pimples or eruptions often appear suddenly on the skin of the horse, and especially in the spring of the year. The disease most frequently appears when the skin is irritable, during or after the process of moulting, or when it sympathizes with any disorder of the stomach. It has been known to follow the eating of poisonous herbs or mow-burnt hay, but much oftener it is to be traced to exposure to cold when the skin was previously irritable, and the horse heated by exercise.

If there is simple eruption, without any marked inflammatory action, alteratives should be resorted to. There is no better alternative than that which is in common use—pulverized antimony, nitre, and sulphur. They should be given on several successive nights. The night is better than the morning, because the warmth of the stable will cause the antimony and sulphur to act more powerfully on the skin. The horse should be warmly clothed, half an hour's walking exercise should be given, an additional rug thrown over him, such green feed as can be procured should be used in moderate quantities, and the chill should be taken from the water.

Should the eruption continue, or assume a more violent character, bleeding and aloes must be had recourse to, but neither should be carried to any extreme. The physic having set, the alteratives should again be had recourse to, and attention should be paid to the comfort and diet of the horse.

Warts.

There are some caustics available, but frequently they must be removed by an operation. If the root is very small, it may be snipped asunder close to the skin with a pair of scissors, and touched with the lunar caustic. If the pedicle or stem is somewhat larger, a ligature of wax silk should be passed firmly round it, and tightened every day.

Rabies, or Madness.

This is a fearful disease of the nervous system. It results from the bite of a rabid animal, and, most commonly, of the companion and friend of the horse, the coach dog. The horse goes out to his usual work, and, for a certain time and distance, performs it as well as he has been accustomed to do; then he stops all at once, trembles, heaves, paws, staggers, and falls.

When the disease can be clearly connected with a previous bite, the sooner the animal is destroyed the better, for *there is no cure*. If the symptoms bear considerable resemblance to rabies, although no bite is suspected, the horse should at least be slung, and the medicine, if any is administered, given in the form of a drink, and with the hand well protected; for if it should be scratched in balling the horse, or the skin should have been previously broken, the saliva of the animal is capable of communicating the disease.

If a horse is bitten by a dog under suspicious circumstances, he should be carefully examined, and every wound, and even the slightest scratch, well burned with the lunar caustic, (nitrate of silver.) The scab should be removed, and the operation repeated on the third day. The hot iron does not answer so well, and other caustics are not so manageable. The caustic must reach every part of the wound; also give half an ounce of spirits ammonia in some warm water sweetened; repeat every thirty minutes until perspiration starts.

Galls on Horses.

Wash with Castile soap and warm water. The following is an excellent recipe for an ointment for wounds and sores of all kinds, and for horses when galled by the saddle or collar, and also for broken chilblains. Take of

Honey,	twelve ounce.
Beeswax,	four ounces.
Burgundy Pitch,	six ounces.
Sweet oil,	half pint.

Melt them together over a slow fire; rub the parts affected; heat it in with a hot iron.

Cracked Heels.

First soak in chamber-lye, then use the above ointment.

OF MANAGING HORSES. 105

ANOTHER OINTMENT FOR CRACKED HEELS OR OLD SORES.

Hog's lard,	one pound.
Beeswax,	four ounces.
Turpentine,	half pound.
Burgundy Pitch,	half pound.
Resin,	half pound.
Honey,	half pound.

Simmer together, then add four ounces spirits turpentine; stir until cool. This is the best ointment for old sores I ever tried.

Colic.

The appearance of this disease may be known from the coldness of the horse's ears and legs, and by his general uneasiness, getting up and laying down often, looking around at his flanks, etc.

The aromatic spirits of ammonia, one or two ounces, dissolved in a pint of warm water, is a good remedy; to be followed by linseed oil, half pint, sweet spirits nitre, half pint, in warm water, sweetened.

To prevent Contagion.

Nail a piece of asafœtida in the bottom of the manger; also put a little copperas in the water they drink.

Diarrhea, Dysentery, or Looseness.

Use a strong decoction of white-oak bark every six hours, until relief is found; add black pepper, if you choose.

Sweany.

Take a leather strap, a half inch wide, and two and a half feet long, soak it in spirits turpentine, insert in your needle, made for the purpose, about eighteen inches long; put your needle at the top of the shoulder, and run it down just under the skin, letting it come out at the lower point of the shoulder; tie a large knot in each end, move it twice a day, keeping the shoulder washed with Castile soap and warm water; let it remain from six to ten days, then remove the strap; bathe often in spirits turpentine; do not forget to rub it.

Further remarks on Sweany.

Since I wrote the above I have learned, from experience, that sweany is caused, sometimes, by a strain. The striffin becomes calloused to the bone, then the shoulder begins to perish. In early stages put your knife in the center of the perished place; be sure you cut through the striffin to the bone, then remove the knife and insert a quill, and blow sufficiently strong to remove the striffin from the bone; get in as much wind as possible. Three or four such operations will generally effect a cure.

N. B.—A horse or mule should not be worked while curing the sweany.

Fistula.

Use your seton as in poll evil or sweany; do not forget your soap and water; always keep a sore clean.

Stoppage in the Bowels.

Take aloes one ounce, ginger one ounce; give in the form of a ball, to be followed with half pint of castor oil. Use injections, if necessary, of the same articles.

Stoppage of the Urine.

First cleanse your horse's privates with warm water and Castile soap, then oil with sweet oil; drench with sweet spirits nitre, half pint, in warm water sweetened. Repeat, if necessary, in six hours; if this should fail, use the following ball:

White resin,	one ounce.
Castile soap,	four drachms.
Oil of juniper,	two drachms.
Camphor,	two drachms.
Saltpetre,	four drachms

This is one dose. Repeat if necessary.

Strains and Sprains.

Take one gallon of good brandy or high wine, one pound of gum myrrh, pounded fine, one ounce of cayenne, and put them into a stone jug. Let it stand five or six days, shake it well every day, then it will be fit for use. Bathe the parts affected, rubbing it in well.

N. B.—Never forget the rubbing.

LINIMENT FOR THE ABOVE.

Alcohol,	one quart.
Turpentine,	one pint.
Corrosive sublimate,	one ounce.
Blue stone,	one ounce.
Camphor,	one ounce.
Sweet oil,	half pint.

Shake well. Use with a brush, very carefully.

ANOTHER LINIMENT.

Take old bacon fat and white of eggs. Mix together.

Cancers, how Cured.

Take the heads of red clover, and fill a brass kettle, and boil them in water for one hour; then take them out and fill the kettle again with fresh ones, and boil them as before, in the same liquor. Strain it off, and press the heads to get out all the juice; then simmer it over a slow fire till it is about the consistence of tar, when it will be fit for use. Be careful not to let it burn. When used, it should be spread on a piece of bladder, split and made soft. It is good for cancers and all old sores. If they are very bad, resort to the surgeon's knife; follow with salve made as follows: Take

Beeswax,	one pound.
Salt butter,	one pound.
Turpentine,	one and half pounds.
Balsam fir,	twelve ounces.

Melt and simmer them together; then strain it off into a basin, and keep it for use. This ointment may be used for all fresh wounds.

To relax the Muscles in setting a Bone.

This may be done by bathing the part with warm water, and is much better than the method that is generally practiced, of extending the muscle by the strength of several persons, which weakens the part so much that the bones are liable to get out of place again; besides, the operation causes severe pain to the patient, and much trouble to the operator, which is all obviated by my method. In cases where a joint is put out, or a bone broken, wrap the part in cloths wet with water as hot as it can be borne, and pour on the warm water for a short time, when the muscles will become relaxed, so that the bones may be put in their place with little trouble. After setting, bathe in cold water, to set the muscle, then put on your splinters and bandages to suit your judgment, according to the locality.

Windgalls.

These are mostly on the hind legs; they are not only eyesores, but sometimes lame the horse. The reason why they are mostly on the hind legs is, he usually stands lower behind in his stall; also, he does the heft of his pulling with his hind legs.

CURE.—On the first appearance of a windgall, bathe with vinegar and spirits turpentine, warm, and put a tight bandage round it. If this does not remove it, lay it open with a knife, and dress it as a common wound.

A new mode to Cast a Horse.

Take two pieces of joist, five or six feet long, lay them about four feet apart, then get some stout plank, seven or eight feet long, and spike them to the joist; be sure it is well done; stand it on its edge, then lead a well horse along side; mark and bore holes, so as to pass a strap through, buckling each and every leg to the platform; then the body, by the loins, and next, to the foreshoulders; also, be sure to confine the head by a nosehalter, so the animal can not raise his head when lying on his side; now your board is fit for use; now attach the horse you intend to operate upon to this platform, or surgeon's board, as we call it; be sure he is firmly confined; be sure to have help enough to lower the board and horse with ease, or hold it in any position you wish to have him in for the operation you intend to perform.

To Dock or Nick a Horse.

Set four posts in the ground, some taller than a horse; halve on your cap-pieces very firm; spike a few planks to its sides; now lead your horse into the stocks thus prepared; put a sling under him, so he can not lie down; make him fast with the halter to the cap in front; then strap each foot to the side planks below; now lay a block of wood on his left hip, draw the tail across it; place a sharp tool, made for the purpose, across the tail, and, with one blow with a maul, sever it; then stop the blood, by searing it with a hot iron. If you wish to nick your horse, take your knife in the right hand, and cut the cord on the right side of the tail in several places; be careful you do not touch the bone, cutting as small a hole in the flesh or skin as possible; then take the knife in the left hand, cutting the left cord, precisely as you have the right; then release him from the stocks, and put him in the pulleys; rest, wash, and anoint, as your judgment may dictate. In case of broken legs, or severe lameness, the sling is very beneficial.

Water-founder, how Cured.

Tie a cord around the tail of your horse, as tight as possible; put a small boy on his back; let him move in a slow trot, for an hour, or less; let the string remain on his tail for ten or twelve hours, then take the string off; in the course of three or four days you may put him to work with safety. One might think this an old woman's whim. I only ask a trial; then no one can doubt.

Corn, or Chest-founder, how Cured.

Take from four to six quarts of blood from the neck vein, as soon as possible; then take one ounce of cayenne, one ounce of gum myrrh, one ounce of gum aloes, one ounce of fine bayberry bark; mix with lard; divide in three parts; give one part immediately, another in twelve hours, the balance in twelve more, in the form of balls. In two or three weeks your horse will be fit to work.

Burst, Rupture, or Pus, how Cured.

After fastening the horse to the surgeon's board, lay him in a position so as the bowels shall fall from the part affected; have your threads made ten or twelve inches long; cut the skin open; be very careful not to cut the bowels; skiver each edge where the flesh is torn; use a hooked needle; put your threads in from the inside, leaving them until they are all in; one inch apart will do; then commence and tie each one by itself; let the ends hang out; proceed the same way with the skin; set the stitches half way between those in the flesh; cut the threads off, leaving them about two inches long; be sure to hitch your horse so he can not gnaw out the stitches; bathe with Castile soap and warm water, night and morning; anoint with the ointment until healed. (If in summer, put a plaster over the wound, leaving a hole through it for the matter to run out.)

Broken Leg, how Set and Cured.

First, put in place, then take some stout cotton cloth, about two inches wide, any length; moisten in warm tar, or resin; bandage well, then place your splints on every side, laying a little cotton under, to prevent galling the leg; then strap them firmly; now take some pieces of timber, shaped to the leg, strap them on so as to let them run one inch below the hoof, so the horse will rest on the timbers, and not on the hoof; hitch your horse so he can not gnaw the lacings; sling him, if necessary; bathe with chamber-lye.

Stifle, or Hip bone, how Set.

Relax the muscle with warm water, as previously described, then let your assistant draw the foot back gently; place your shoulder against the front part of the bone, your hands each side of the thigh. Lift gently until it comes into place; retain your hold until your assistant brings the foot forward; do not back the horse if you can help it. Bathe in cold water; put a rolling shoe on the well foot, so he will stand on the lame one.

How to make a Rolling Shoe.

Take a common shoe and put two straps of hoop-iron on the bottom, so it will be rounding on the bottom, that the horse may not stand his whole weight on the well foot. Do not forget to put this shoe on the well foot.

Gravel, how Cured.

If your horse should get graveled, cut it out if possible, and fill the place with hot tar. If you can not get at it with the knife, it will work out itself in time; if you find it is coming out at the top of the hoof, cut the skin, for it is hard to work through it.

If the horse steps on an old nail, or other metal, and lames himself, be sure and get it out; dress it with spirits of turpentine; fill the cavity with hot tar; do not forget to grease the nail, or other metal, and put it in the fire, as it will save much pain; this may seem a whim; it is but a little trouble.

I once was called on to dress a man's hand that was sawed badly by an old saw. It pained him much; he was cold, and chills ran over him. Some one suggested that the saw should be brought in and greased, and laid by the fire; when this was done, he got easy at once. I have tried it often since, and find it has a good effect.

Hoof-bound, how Cured.

Soak the feet in chamber-lye, and press the heels of the shoes apart with the tongs; some use the screw shoe, and screw the heels apart; you can do as you please.

Hide-bound, how Cured.

Give your horse a little blood-root (fine) in his feed. A table-spoonful once a day will do no harm.

How to Castrate or Guild a Horse.

First, fasten him to the surgeon's board, as described in my new mode of casting. Place him in a position to suit your convenience; get directly behind him, take the lower stone or testicle in your left hand, make the incision with a knife, in your right hand; make it long, for there is danger in its healing too quick; then peel the meat of the stone or testicle out; do not cut it off square or short, but scrape the string from the stone, until you scrape it off; leave the string long, if you wish the horse to retain the pride of the stallion; if you cut the string short, he will be forever dull, sluggish, and lazy. Now treat the other in the same form. Wash well with salt and water; keep him in a dry place, to prevent his taking cold; if he should take cold and maturate badly, syringe the wound with warm water and molasses. This is very good in case of fly-blows.

Feed your horse on bruised oats, and the best of hay, not forgetting to give bran mash once a day.

How to select and treat a Horse on a Journey.

First, select a horse that is well and hearty; not too poor, for he will be weak, or too fat, as a fat horse will not last; select one that has been fed on hard food, had plenty of exercise, not too much; do not drive him too far the first day, or too fast when you first start; allow your horse to wet his mouth often, not allowing him to drink too much at a time; do not allow him to be fed when too warm; be sure and see that he is fed and properly attended; see that his stall is dry and well littered, that he may rest well for the night; in cold or damp weather, do not forget the blanket, and see he has it on; hand rubbing is excellent to prevent his legs from swelling; drive slow up hill, drive gently down hill; if you are in a hurry, press the horse on the plain, or where the road is not too steep or too sloping; if you discover your horse wishes to stop, do not let him stop of his own accord, but stop him yourself. Although he may be half way up a steep hill, it is better for you to stop the horse, than allow him to stop without the word.

Before I conclude this chapter, I will give you the horse's address to his rider, (from Mr. Bracken's treatise) which is well worth observation.

> Up the hill, spur me not;
> Down the hill, ride me not;
> On the plain, spare me not;
> To the ostler, trust me not.

To remove Fly-blows from a Sore.

Wash in molasses and warm water; you will be surprised to see how soon it will have an effect. I once saw a young colt completely covered with fly-blows; it was thought, by those who saw him, that he would die; I had him washed with molasses and water two or three times in the course of the day; the next morning he seemed to be perfectly well, and free from fly blows.

Cold, how Cured.

First, wrap with warm blankets, with a good litter; feed light on bruised oats and long hay; water often; give a table-spoonful of the following compound in their oats, three times a day. Take of

Aniseed powder,	four ounces.
Ferugreek,	four ounces.
Liquorice powder,	four ounces.
Elecampane powder,	four ounces.
Flour of brimstone,	four ounces.

Scours, how Cured.

Take of

Rhubarb, in powder,	one ounce.
Gum myrrh, in powder,	half ounce.
Saffron,	half ounce.
Ginger, in powder,	two ounces.
Bayberry bark, in powder,	two ounces.

Make in ball, with lard. Give one-third every twelve hours.

Scratches, and their Cure.

This disease in a horse is like the itch on a person. It sometimes causes lameness. Anoint with the following ointment. Take

Hog's lard,	one pound.
Burgundy Pitch,	two ounces.
Beeswax,	two ounces.
Flour of brimstone,	one ounce.
Red precipitate,	one ounce.

Simmer over a slow fire; then add two ounces spirits turpentine. Stir till cold.

Lampas.

The palate of the young horse is more subject to inflammation than the old. The bars of the mouth sometimes swell below the surface of the teeth, and become very painful when feeding, and the horse loses flesh. Every one has their own cure. Within the last six years I have burned them out, with an iron made for that purpose. The horse should have mash feed for a few days, then he can have hard food again.

Harnesses.

We have said a great deal about horses, in this treatise, both of our own experience and the experience of others. I will say a few words concerning the harness that holds this noble animal in subjection.

It has been the practice of our stables to wash and oil harness so often as to rot it, and it becomes a useless thing. I will here give you a recipe for cleaning harness, so it will last long, and will not catch the dust. Take

Castile soap,	one pound.
Beeswax,	two ounces.
Gum arabic,	two ounces.
Olive, or sweet oil,	one pint.
Alcohol,	one pint.
Drop black, pulverized,	one and a half ounces.
Indigo, "	half ounce.

Simmer the first four together; add the rest when partly cool.

Clean your harness with this preparation. Use no oil. You may use warm water and Castile soap, if you choose. Polish with a woolen rag.

INDEX.

PART I.
THE ORIENTAL ART THE TRUE PHILOSOPHY.

	PAGE
How to make a horse pace,	7
How to cure a horse from interfering,	7
How to shoe horses,	8
Early training,	8
Taming a vicious horse,	11
Teaching a horse various tricks,	16
To make a horse lie down,	20
How to make a horse follow you,	21
Breaking colts,	21
Kicking,	24
Slipping the halter,	26
Restlessness while being shod,	27
To prevent rolling in the stall,	27
How to break horses from balking,	28
Crib biting,	29
To make a horse lie down at night,	29
Unwillingness to be mounted,	29
Running away,	30
Restiveness,	30
Biting,	31
The author's fancy for a trick horse,	31
How to succeed in getting the colt from pasture,	32
How to stable a colt without trouble,	33
Time to reflect,	34
The kind of halter,	35
Remarks on the horse,	35
Experiments with the robe,	36
Suppositions on the sense of smelling,	37
Prevailing opinion of horsemen,	38
Powel's system of approaching the colt,	40
Remarks on Powel's treatment how to govern horses of any kind,	43
How to proceed if your horse is of a stubborn disposition,	46
How to halter and lead the colt,	47
How to lead a colt by the side of a broken horse,	50
How to lead a colt into the stable and hitch him without having him pull on the halter,	51
The kind of bit and how to accustom a horse to it,	53
How to saddle a colt,	53
How to mount the colt,	55
How to ride a colt,	57
The proper way to bit a colt,	59
How to drive a horse that is very wild and has any vicious habits,	60
Further remarks on balking,	62
To break a horse to harness,	67
How to hitch a horse in a sulky,	67
How to make a horse stand without holding,	68

(119)

PART II.

THE GENERAL MANAGEMENT OF THE HORSE.

	PAGE		PAGE
Breeding horses,	71	Food,	80
The horse in the stable,	74	The sense of smell,	88
Air,	75	Management of the feet,	89
Grooming,	77	Points of a good horse,	91
Light,	78	The age of horses after the ninth year,	91
Exercise,	79		
Litter,	80	Age of horses by the teeth,	92

PART III.

DISEASES AND THEIR CURE.

	PAGE		PAGE
To mix and give a ball,	93	Cancers, how cured,	108
Glanders,	94	To relax the muscles in setting a bone,	108
Diseases of the teeth,	94		
Inflammation of the eye,	95	Windgalls,	109
Lung fever,	95	A new mode to cast a horse,	109
Distemper, how cured,	96	To dock or nick a horse,	110
Condition powders,	96	Water-founder, how cured,	110
Heaves,	96	Corn, or chest-founder, how cured,	111
String halt,	97		
Caution,	98	Burst, rupture, or pus, how cured,	111
Poll evil,	98		
Strangles,	98	Broken leg, how set and cured,	112
Bots,	99		
Tetanus or Lock-jaw,	99	Stifle, or hip bone, how set,	112
Mange,	100	How to make a rolling shoe,	112
Surfeit,	102	Gravel, how cured,	112
Warts,	103	Hoof-bound, how cured,	113
Rabies, or madness,	103	Hide-bound, how cured,	113
Galls on horses,	104	How to castrate or guild a horse,	113
Cracked heels,	104		
Colic,	105	How to select and treat a horse on a journey,	114
To prevent contagion,	105		
Diarrhea, dysentery, etc.,	105	To remove fly-blows from a sore,	115
Sweany,	105		
Further remarks on sweany,	106	Cold, how cured,	115
Fistula,	106	Scours, how cured,	116
Stoppage in the bowels,	106	Scratches, and their cure,	116
Stoppage of the urine,	107	Lampas,	116
Strains and sprains,	107	Harnesses,	117

www.ingramcontent.com/pod-product-compliance
Lightning Source LLC
Chambersburg PA
CBHW020126170426
43199CB00009B/653